AF552812
JEFFERSON
GEORGETOWN ST.
TODD ST.
HOCKER'S FEMALE COLLEGE.
BIRDS EYE VIEW
OF THE CITY OF
LEXINGTON
FAYETTE COUNTY,
KENTUCKY.
LOOKING
1871.
SOUTH WEST.
CHURCHES:
14. First } Baptist.
15. Second } " "
16. Christian.
17. Episcopal.
18. Methodist North.
19. " " South.
20. First Presbyterian.
21. Second " "
22. Roman Catholic.
23. African Baptist.
24. " " Methodist
AGRICULTURAL & MECHANICAL COLLEGE

The Squire's
SKETCHES OF LEXINGTON

The Squire's SKETCHES

Lexington's First Streetcar (1890)

1972
Lexington

OF LEXINGTON

by J. Winston Coleman, Jr.

Published and Distributed
by Henry Clay Press
Lexington, Kentucky 40501

Library of Congress
Number 72-91393

ISBN 87642-009-9

First Edition,
November, 1972
Second Edition,
December, 1972

Designed by
Ed Houlihan

Copyright
Henry Clay Press
1972

To my Nephews
Walter Payne Coleman, Jr.
and
John Howard Coleman

Old Fair Grounds

Contents

Fayette County Hemp Fields

A Tribute

Many future generations will be grateful to Squire Coleman for compiling this chronology of Lexington's first two centuries. The Squire retains, as no other student of Lexington's past, thousands of often minute but important facts collected in a lifetime of pursuing the history of the Bluegrass. Previously chronicled only in his vivid memory, *The Squire's Sketches of Lexington* is a unique history of Lexington, Kentucky.

In publishing this, our fourth Coleman book since Henry Clay Press was born with his *Historic Kentucky* in 1967, we hope to thank Mr. Coleman for his immeasurable contribution to Kentucky history and historians. We trust that we express the gratitude of all citizens of the Commonwealth for the legacy he has given us. We believe *Sketches* will continue to add to it.

The Editors

November 5, 1972

Preface

By the close of the first decade of the nineteenth century, Lexington had become the center of the rich Bluegrass region of Kentucky and was the most important town in the Western Country. It was one of the first cultural centers to develop after the Revolutionary War and soon became known as the "Athens of the West." From the early 1780s to 1820, Lexington was the largest and wealthiest town west of the Alleghenies with the exception of the French city of New Orleans. Transylvania University established Lexington as a national educational center.

The great fertility of the Bluegrass land, coupled with the industriousness of the pioneers who came to settle it, brought about a prosperity and culture still visible in Lexington today, nearly 195 years later.

One traveler, Henry B. Fearon, estimated the factory investment in Lexington in 1817 at two and one quarter million dollars. It was, he thought, "all the more remarkable in that Lexington lay some fifteen miles from the Kentucky River, the closest navigable stream." There were in this period, ac-

Third Courthouse, 1806-1883

Masterson's Station

cording to Fearon, "three tobacco factories, four coach factories, several gun-powder mills, a lead factory, and founderies for casting iron and brass, together with a number of places for making cotton and hempen yarns."

Lexington, the early market and manufacturing center of the Western Country, found itself commercially isolated when the steamboat became the most practical carrier for passengers and freight. Not being located closer to a navigable river, she lost much of her commercial importance. When the steamboat *Enterprise* in 1815, made its maiden voyage upstream from New Orleans to Louisville, the Bluegrass capital was forced to surrender the major share of her trade to the raparian cities of Louisville and Cincinnati. By 1830, the Athens of the West was almost completely shorn of its commercial glory, and settled down to become a cultural and intellectual city rather than a great industrial center. Lexington was yet the seat of Fayette County, one of the three original Kentucky counties, created in 1780 by the Virginia legislature.

In the preparation of this work the author acknowledges assistance from a number of sources, his thanks being especially due to Edward T. Houlihan III, Holman Hamilton, H. Joseph Houlihan, Clyde T. Burke, John A. Womack, Jr., Hambleton Tapp, Daniel M. Bowmar, Sr., Boynton Merrill, Jr., Mrs. Robert P. Wooley, Miss Roemol Henry and Fred Bryant. Sincere thanks are extended to Burton Milward for reading and checking the manuscript and for offering a number of valuable suggestions and related materials which have greatly improved each chapter.

It is hoped that the reader may find in these pages a clearer view of the events that transpired in the life of Lexington which, as William Faux so rightly prophesied in 1823, "will continue to flourish when other cities fade and die . . . "

J. Winston Coleman, Jr.

June 15, 1972
2048 Blairmore Road

The Squire's
SKETCHES OF LEXINGTON

1772-1789

The Birth of the Frontier Town

Overshadowed at first by Boonesborough, Harrodsburg, Bryan's Station, and the other frontier settlements, this period saw Lexington begin to become the center of government, education, and commerce in the Western Country. Still one of the Virginia counties, the area was spurred on by the establishment of Transylvania University and the *Kentucky Gazette* during these early years.

1772

The Watauga Association was organized this year in North Carolina, with Colonel Richard Henderson, the chief proprietor. As a result of this movement, the town of Boonesborough on the Kentucky River was established and the foundation of the Transylvania Colony laid on April 2, 1775.

Fincastle County was created by an act of the Virginia legislature out of Botetourt County. The new county included all of Kentucky and the site of the future town of Lexington.

1773

Robert McAfee and party were exploring the wilderness of Central Kentucky in search of cane lands. Daniel Boone was also in this area and probably passed over the site of Lexington.

1774

The site of Lexington first appears in a written record on April 19, 1774, when Lord Dunmore, governor of Virginia, signed a military warrant for 200 acres "near the head of the middle fork of Elkhorn" to Sergeant James Buford, for services in the French and Indian War.

1775

During the summer, a party of eight pioneers from Harrod's Fort (Harrodsburg), came to the central Bluegrass to establish a settlement north of the Kentucky River. They camped near a large spring, known as the Wilderness or McConnell's Spring, which was located on the south side of the Old Frankfort Pike on the grounds of the present-day Central Rock Company. Here, on June 4, or 5, 1775, the pioneers, while sitting around their camp fire, named the future settlement "Lexington," in honor of the first battle of the American Revolution.[1] A small cabin was erected by William McConnell (later his station), but due to Indian threats no settlement was made, and the party returned to the safety of Harrod's Fort.[2]

1776

Kentucky County was created by the Virginia legislature out of Fincastle County, October, 1776, to commence December 1, 1776. This county included most of Kentucky and the future site of Lexington.

On December 29, McClelland's Fort at Georgetown was attacked by a band of 40 to 50 Indians, several of whom were killed, including Chief Pluggy. John McClelland and Charles White of the fort were killed. McClelland's Fort (Royal Spring) was abandoned and the men returned to Harrodsburg which, with St. Asaph's (Stanford) and Boonesborough, were the only garrisons in Kentucky.

1777

Harrodsburg became the seat of Kentucky County, Virginia.

Indians continued to harass the Kentucky settlements during the months of March through July.

1778

The year before Lexington became a permanent settlement, Fort Boonesborough on the Kentucky River (in present-day Madison County) was attacked by the French-Canadian officer Dequindre with ten white companions and 400 Indians. This force appeared

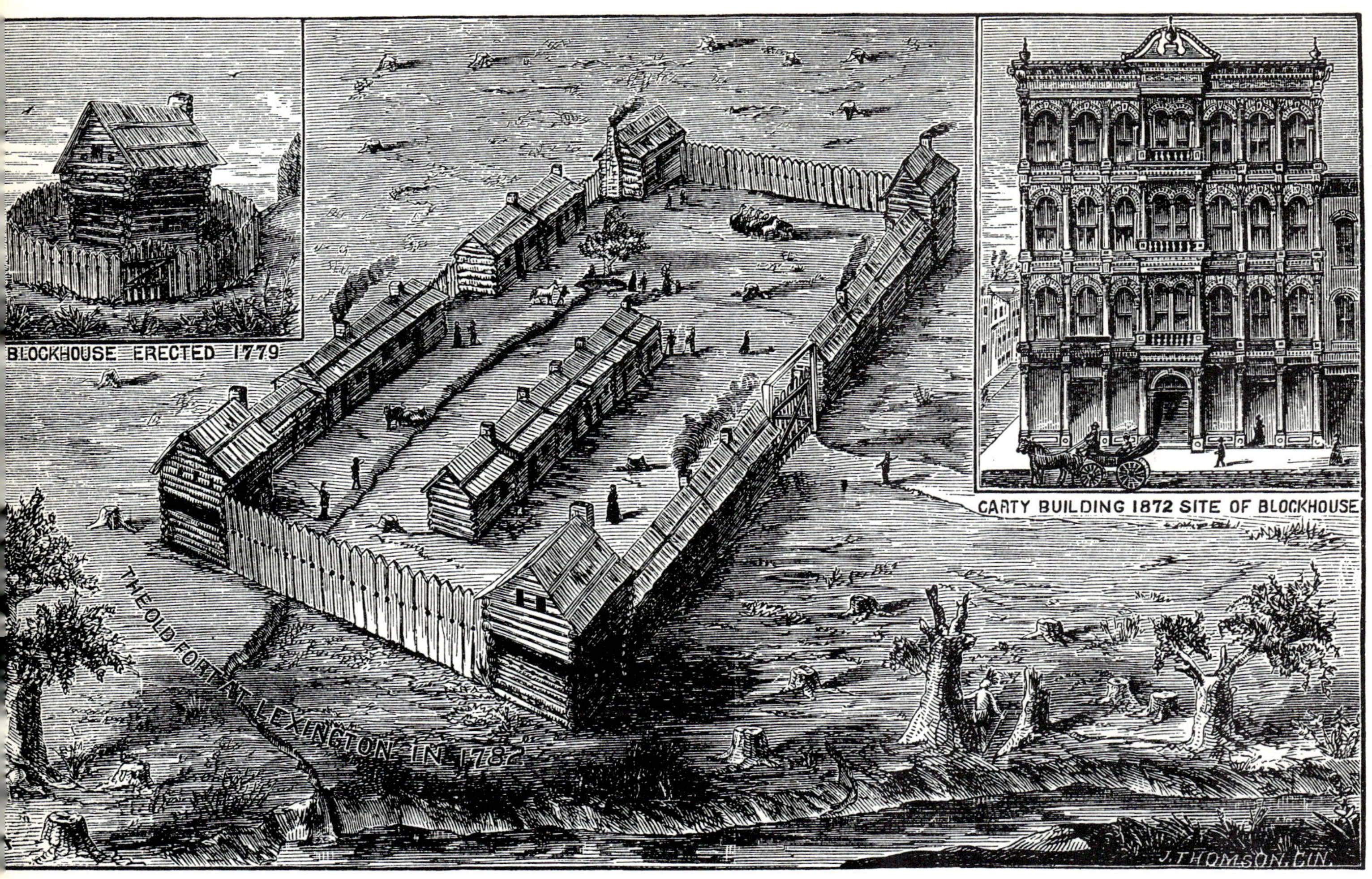

A line etching from George W. Ranck's History of Lexington *published in 1872 shows an artist's conception of the Lexington fort in 1782. The Carty Building in the inset was built and owned by Ranck's father-in-law and is described on page 87.*

before the gates of the fort on September 7, 1778, and demanded that Daniel Boone surrender his post. This was refused and the Indians laid siege. The defenders of the fort held out for 13 days, after which the enemy retreated in complete disgust.

1779

Robert Patterson, an ensign in Capt. Levi Todd's company, was ordered "to establish a garrison at some convenient site north of the Kentucky River." Accordingly, on April 17, 1779, Patterson with 25 men from Harrod's Fort began the erection of a stockade on the site of Lexington.[3] This garrison was built in the shape of a parallelogram, two sides of which were the back walls of cabins, while the spaces in between were filled with sharpened posts set in the ground, ten feet high. An unfailing spring was within the walls of the stockade, which stood on the south side of Main Street (site of J. D. Purcell building), about midway between Broadway and Mill streets. Josiah Collins, one of Patterson's party, stated: "We went to Lexington and built a block house [stockade], commencing on the 17th of April," and "we cleared about 30 acres of land that season and planted some corn."[4] Lexington was permanently established this year.

1780

In January, forty-seven settlers met and agreed to lay out the future town of Lexington, to be divided into eighty-seven "Inn Lotts" and sixty-five "Out Lotts."[5] Those close in were to contain one-third of an acre, and the out-lots to have five acres each. Later in the same year Main Street was laid off, which necessitated demolishing the wooden stockade extending diagonally across it. With the garrison gone, the little village was without protection.

In June, Captain Henry Bird of "his Majesty's 8th Regiment of Foot," with a number of Canadians and Great Lakes Indians, captured Ruddell's and Martin's stations, the two pioneer stations in Central Kentucky. Bird used a three- and a six-pound cannon against the stockades. Citizens of the infant settlement of Lexington were greatly alarmed, knowing they could not withstand an artillery attack.

Fayette, Jefferson and Lincoln counties were created by the Virginia legislature out of Kentucky County, November 1, 1780. Fayette County was named for the Revolutionary War general, the Marquis de Lafayette, who came from France to aid the young colonies in their struggle against England.

Transylvania University was chartered in 1780 by the Virginia legislature, to establish "a public school or seminary of learning." The infant school was slow in getting started and on February 1, 1785, the first session of the Transylvania Seminary began in the log house of "Father" David Rice, a Presbyterian minister, in Boyle County, several miles from Danville. On June 1, 1789, the classes of Transylvania Seminary were transferred to Lexington.

1781

In April, Col. John Todd "erected a new fort upon a very advantageous situation at this place [Lexington]," and made it "proof against swivels and small artillery, which so terrify our people." The fort was built upon the plan of a quadrangle, "80 feet square in the clear. Walls 7 feet thick of rammed dirt enclosed in good timber, nine feet high, from 4 feet upwards 5 feet thick, and proof against small arms."[6] There was a moat 5 feet deep around the fort, and a magazine for storage of powder within the walls. This fort replaced the earlier wooden stockade which stood on the south side of Main Street, between Mill and Broadway.

Daniel Boone was a representative to the General Assembly of Virginia, from the newly formed county of Fayette. On June 21, he presented a petition[7] to the House of Representatives, "signed by sundry inhabitants of the county of Fayette, whose names are thereunto subscribed," praying that "the town of Lexington in the said county, may be established a town, by Act of Assembly."[8] Thus Boone, the old pioneer, was instrumental in securing a charter for the infant town of Lexington.

1782

By an act of the General Assembly of Virginia, a tract of 710 acres in Fayette County was vested in seven trustees and established as a town by the name of Lexington, May 6, 1782.

In the spring, Fayette County's first courthouse was erected at the northwest corner of Main and Broadway. It was a two-story structure "built of logs rived with a whip saw,"[9] and contained "two rooms on each floor, eighteen feet square, with fire places in each, and two good dry cellars, each eighteen feet square."[10] John Bradford later used this building as the printing office of his *Kentucky Gazette* and described it as "the excellent stand at the corner of Main and [Main] Cross Streets, Lexington, known by the name of the old courthouse."[11]

Captain William Caldwell, with a force of Indians and Canadians attacked and laid siege to Bryan's Station, six miles north of Lexington, on August 15 to 17, 1782. Unsuccessful in their attempt, Captain Caldwell and his Indian forces withdrew to engage in the Battle of Lower Blue Licks, two days later, on August 19, 1782. The Kentuckians suffered a memorable defeat in this, the last battle of the American Revolution.

Transylvania's first building (described at left) was Father David Rice's Boyle County cabin several miles from Danville.

Patterson Cabin (described below) was returned to Lexington through the efforts of Governor A. B. Chandler and Scientist Charles Allen Thomas, both Transylvania alumni.

1783

William McConnell was one of the 12 or 15 men who had camped in 1775 around the big spring known as the Wilderness or McConnell's Spring. Here, in 1783, he erected a small station. This spring was, at an early day, the favorite resort of the people of Lexington on public occasions. McConnell's Station was later abandoned and the settlers merged with the infant town of Lexington. John Filson's map of 1784 shows "McConnel's Sta. and Mill" to be on this site, southwest of Lexington on the Old Frankfort Pike and west of the James E. Pepper Distillery.

In June, schoolteacher John McKinney had an encounter with a wildcat which had entered his classroom on the Public Square. After quite a struggle, McKinney strangled the animal with his bare hands.

The log house of Col. Robert Patterson, founder of Lexington and Cincinnati, stood at 331 Patterson Street in 1783. This log cabin was removed to Dayton, Ohio, in 1901, and later returned to the Transylvania University campus, where it was rededicated on June 5, 1939. This one-room cabin is thought to have been one of the first houses erected in Lexington.

John Filson's 1784 map of the West.

1784

The Rev. Adam Rankin of Virginia built a small Presbyterian church, Mount Zion Church, on the present site of the University

The Adam Rankin House before it was moved in 1971 to South Mill Street to avoid destruction in the wake of a new bank.

of Kentucky Experiment Station on South Limestone Street, opposite Virginia Avenue. This was the first church of any kind in Lexington. Rankin was "deposed" from the Presbyterian Church in October, 1792, over the use of Watts Psalms in public worship. He later took part of his congregation with him into the Associate Reformed Presbyterian Church.

General James Wilkinson, soldier of the Revolutionary War, migrated west and in 1784 opened the first store in Lexington. His goods were transported from Philadelphia to Pittsburgh by wagon, flat-boated down the Ohio River to Limestone (Maysville), and carried on pack horses to Lexington. In addition, Wilkinson carried on an extensive commerce between Kentucky and New Orleans, shipping produce by the river route to the Crescent City. He became a key figure in a plot to induce the southwest United States to form a separate nation allied to Spain.

The Adam Rankin House, which stood at 215 West High Street, is said to be the oldest house in Lexington. Built in 1784, it was the early home of the Reverend Rankin, pioneer Presbyterian minister. The structure was also the residence of Samuel D. McCullough, a noted astronomer, author and mathematician. Nathan Burrows in the 1830s conducted an academy here and was the inventor of a superior brand of table mustard. Burrows' "Lexington Mustard" became a famous product throughout the country.

John Filson, land speculator and schoolteacher in Lexington, published his rare book, entitled *The Discovery, Settlement, and Present State of Kentucke,* in an edition of 1,500 copies. This small 118-page volume with map was printed in 1784 by James Adams, in Wilmington, Delaware. This is the rarest of all Kentucky books and not more than a dozen copies are known to have survived. Filson's work was not a true history; it was an emigrants' guide to the Western Country. Filson was killed by Indians while on a surveying trip on the Little Miami River in Ohio.

1785

Although Lexington was one of the earliest settlements of Kentucky, it was not until 1785 that it assumed the appearance of a frontier village. At this time it consisted of three rows of log cabins.

On May 11, the town trustees held their first meeting of the year and issued deeds for "Inn Lotts" to Evan Francis, Simon West, Casper Carsner and Percival Butler.

1786

The first Baptist church in Lexington was constituted in July, 1786, as the Town Fork Baptist Church. Three years later a little band of Baptists erected a log meeting house on the "old Baptist burial grounds" on West Main Street, west of Felix Street.[12] This group, pastored by the Reverend John Gano, worshipped here until a permanent brick church was erected in 1819 on North Mill Street, near Third Street. About this time the church was reorganized as the First Baptist Church.

Ellerslie (described on page 90) was built by Levi Todd about 1787 and served as the home of leaders of the western city until the Lexington Water Company purchased the land in 1884. It was occupied until the mid-1930's and was razed in 1947-48.

Captain Thomas Young operated a tavern on Upper Street facing the courthouse and for many years maintained a reputation for hospitality.

1787

John Bradford and his brother Fielding established the *Kentucky Gazette.* The Bradford brothers visited Philadelphia where they acquired a rudimentary knowledge of the printing art and purchased a small hand press and a scanty supply of type. This was floated down the Ohio River to Maysville and hauled to Lexington over "Smith's waggon-road." On August 11, 1787, John Bradford drew the first issue of the *Kentucky Gazette* from the forms. A back room of the log courthouse at Main Street and Broadway was used as the printing office for Kentucky's first newspaper and the second in the Western Country. *The Gazette* ceased publication in 1848.

1788

The city fathers ordered John Coburn and Samuel Blair "to have a bridge or causeway built across Town Branch at Main Cross [Broadway] Street," and several years later a committee was appointed "to make log bridges across the canal at Mulberry [Limestone], Upper and Mill streets." The middle fork of Elkhorn, known as Town Branch, ran through the central part of the infant settlement and often overflowed from its banks.

On November 17, a charter was issued by the Grand Lodge of Virginia to Richard C. Anderson, Green Clay, John Fowler and others "to hold a regular lodge of Free Masons at the town of Lexington, in the District of Kentucky, by the name, title and designation of Lexington Lodge No. 25."[13] This first lodge in the Western Country met in a log cabin at the northeast corner of Walnut and Short streets. When the Grand Lodge of Kentucky was formed in 1800, the name of this pioneer lodge was changed to Lexington Lodge No. 1, F. & A. M., by which it is known today.

Lexington's second courthouse and the first on the present site, adjacent to the "public square" or Cheapside, was completed in the fall of 1788.[14] This structure was a two-story stone building facing Main Street, with four rooms and a hallway on each floor; the whole building "was covered in with a clap board roof." This early temple of justice was razed in 1806 to make way for a new brick courthouse on the same site.

1789

Early in 1789, a small group of Methodists began holding services in a log house at the southwest corner of Short and Deweese streets, where the First Baptist Church now stands. In 1814, Maddox Fisher sold the property to the Methodist trustees, describing it as "All that part of Out Lott No. 23, on which the Methodist meeting-house now stands." The congregation met here until 1819.

Robert Sanders, a Lexington distiller, offered a reward of twenty pounds or 100 gallons of "prime whiskey" for the return of his runaway slave. Whiskey was useful as money, for which it frequently served as substitute in frontier commerce.[15]

The Lexington Light Infantry, the oldest military company in Kentucky, was organized in Lexington in 1789 as a measure against Indian attacks. Gen. James Wilkinson, veteran of the Revolutionary War, was elected first captain. Resplendent in their bright uniforms of blue coats and blue pantaloons with black hats and red plumes, the company used the level ground at Maxwell Spring for their political rallies, militia musters and drills. This company supplied many officers and men for the Indian wars, War of 1812, Mexican and Civil War.

David Humphreys, who designed and made the first seal of the Commonwealth of Kentucky, advertised in the *Kentucky Gazette* that he lived near the courthouse at the "Sign of the Buffalo" where he repaired clocks and watches. He made the 41 survey plates used by James Hughes in *Hughes' Reports,* the first publication (Lexington, 1803) carrying the various decisions of Kentucky's first Supreme Court.

Notes

1. *The Reporter,* Lexington, July 29, 1809.
2. Perrin, *History of Fayette County,* p. 223.
3. *The American Pioneer,* Vol. II, p. 346.
4. Draper Mss. 12CC65. Interview with Josiah Collins.
5. Hening, *The Statutes at Large,* Vol. X, pp. 315-17.
6. Col. John Todd to Governor Jefferson of Virginia. Draper Mss. 11S202.
7. Original petition in the Virginia State Library, Richmond.
8. *Virginia House Journal,* 1781, p. 27.
9. Draper Mss. 11CC164. John D. Shane interview with Ned Darnaby.
10. *Kentucky Gazette,* January 16, 1800.
11. *Ibid.,* January 16, 1800.
12. Site of the present First Baptist Church, 535 West Main Street.
13. Coleman, *Masonry in the Bluegrass,* pp. 27-31.
14. Coleman, *The Court-Houses of Lexington,* pp. 11, 12.
15. *Kentucky Gazette,* June 13, 1789.

1790-1809

Two Decades of "Firsts" in the West

[NUMB. IV] THE [VOL. II.]

KENTUCKE GAZETTE,

SATURDAY, SEPTEMBER 20, 1788.

LEXINGTON: *Printed by* JOHN BRADFORD *at his* OFFICE *in Main Street, where Subſcriptions, Advertiſements, &c. for this paper, are thankfully received, and* PRINTING *in its different branches done with Care and Expedition*

EXTRACTS from the Journals of a CONVENTION held at Danville *the Twenty eighth day of July, 1788.*

RESOLVED,

WHEREAS it appears to the members of this Convention, That the United States in Congreſs Aſſembled, have for the preſent declined to ratify the compact entered into between the Legiſlature of Virginia and the people of this Diſtrict reſpecting the erection of the Diſtrict into an independent State; in conſequence of which the powers veſted in this convention are diſſolved, and whatever orders or reſolution they paſs cannot be conſidered as having any legal force or obligation: but being anxious for the ſafety and proſperity of ourſelves and Conſtituents, do earneſtly recommend to the good people inhabiting the ſeveral counties within the Diſtrict each to elect five Repreſentatives on the times of holding their Courts in the month of October next, to meet at Danville on the firſt Monday in November following; to continue in Office until the firſt day of January 1790; and that they delegate to their ſaid Repreſentatives full powers to take ſuch meaſures for obtaining admiſſion of the Diſtrict as a ſeparate and independent member of the United States of America, and the navigation of the River Miſſiſſippi, as may appear moſt conducive to thoſe important purpoſes: and alſo to form a Conſtitution of Government for the Diſtrict, and organize the ſame when they ſhall judge it neceſſary, or

SALT

TO BE EXCHANGED FOR

TOBACCO

in Lexington, by *JAMES WILKINSON.*

Auguſt 1, 1788.

TAKEN up on the Rolling Fork of Salt River, Nelſon County, about the twelfth of June laſt, a bay mare (with a laſt ſprings colt about thirteen hands and a half high, neither dockt nor branded, four years old laſt ſpring: Poſted and appraiſed to Nine Pounds. *BENJAMIN HEAD.*

TWO DOLLARS REWARD.

STrayed from the ſubſcriber in Lexington, about the firſt of this month, a young bay Horſe, two years old laſt ſpring, about fourteen hands high, has a ſmall ſtar in his forehead, branded on the buttock with a pot-hook; any perſon that takes up ſaid horſe and delivers him to me ſhall receive the above reward.

TWO DOLLARS

R D.

STrayed from Lexington, about the firſt of June laſt, a bright bay Mare, and a dark bay year old Horſe colt, the Mare four years old laſt ſpring, about fourteen hands high, natural trotter, branded on the near ſhoulder and buttock thus I ap pared to be near foaling; Whoever delivers ſaid Mare to me in Lexington ſhall have the above reward.

Sept. 10, 1788. ROB. PATTERSON.

STrayed away from the ſubſcriber laſt ſpring, a Strawbery roan Mare, about fourteen hands high, three years old laſt ſpring, black mane, tail and legs as high as the knees, a ſmall ſtar in her forehead, trots, not dockt, branded on the near ſhoulder thus ID W o ver delivers ſaid Mare to me near Lexington, ſhall receive Two Dollars rew rd, and reaſonable charges. MOSES DOUGHERTY.

JUST OPENED

The history of the period is filled with "firsts" as the booming western city began to build. The first legislature, library, bank, city directory, post office, college building, and fire company strengthened Lexington's position as the center of frontier commerce. Henry Clay moved to Lexington and opened his law practice as the beginning of his famous career in his adopted state.

1790

The first Methodist Conference west of the Allegheny Mountains was held on May 15, 1790, at Masterson's Station, with Bishop Francis Asbury presiding. The plain, two-story log structure was located about five miles northwest of Lexington on the Leestown Pike where the U.S. Public Service Hospital now stands. This early conference lasted two or three days and was attended by a considerable number of pioneer church people. The old log building, near a big spring, was torn down a number of years ago; a suitable granite marker was recently erected on the site.

In May, 1790, John Bradford organized the first regular fire company in Lexington — the Union Company, which was followed by the Kentuckian, the Lyon Company and the Resolution. The Union Company gave several balls at which admission was charged to purchase supplies and equipment.

Col. James Trotter commanded volunteers from Lexington in General Harman's expedition against the Miami Indians.

George Eads and James Keyes brought the first coal to Lexington from Sturgeon's Creek in Lee County. Their coal was floated in barges down the Kentucky River to Cleveland's Ferry, and hauled to Lexington.

Around 1790, the first Negro church in Kentucky was organized in Lexington as the African Baptist Church; later it became the First Baptist Church. The Rev. Peter Durett, known as "Old Captain," pastored this church from 1790 to 1823, and was followed by the Rev. London Ferrill, who served from 1823 to 1854. Meetings were held for some years in the homes of the church members. Alfred Warner sold the church building at the southwest corner of Short and Deweese to the congregation in 1834. Pleasant Green Church also claims to be the oldest, both congregations having descended from the Rev. Durett's church.

1791

Messrs. Stout and Higbee, local "house joiners," in the summer of 1791 built a two-story brick building, 50 by 25 feet, on the south side of West Main (site of the Purcell Building), between Mill Street and Broadway.[1] Lexington's first market house had five rooms on the ground floor and four on the second; one was 26 by 9 feet "in which the stairs land."[2] The plot of ground was 50 by 212 feet and ran back to Water Street. The ground floor was devoted to the needs of the market house; later the building became known as the State House.

During the summer of 1791, some of the members of Rev. Adam Rankin's Mount Zion Presbyterian Church on South Limestone

Street (site of the U. K. Experiment Station), moved "downtown" and erected a frame meeting house on the east side of North Mill Street, 200 feet south of Short Street. This church was described as being "50 feet long, 40 feet wide, 22 feet high, with a gallery 15 feet wide around 3 squares [sides] of the house." The name of the congregation was then changed to the First Presbyterian Church. The building was not completed at one time, and in 1799 the gallery and cupola were added.

1792

The first Kentucky legislature met on June 4, 1792, on the second floor of the Market House on Main Street, and Isaac Shelby of Lincoln County was inaugurated governor. The first session continued until June 29th, and the second lasted from November 8th through December 22nd. The legislature then bade farewell to Lexington and adjourned "to hold its next session [in 1793] in the house of Andrew Holmes, located on the southwest corner of Wapping and Wilkinson streets, in Frankfort," that town having been selected as the permanent seat of government.

1793

Transylvania University's first building, a two-story brick structure on a stone foundation, was completed and occupied by mid-summer 1793. It closely resembled a typical Georgian residence of the time with large chimneys at either end. The building stood at the north end of the College Square (now Gratz Park) and faced downtown Lexington. It was razed in 1818 to make way for the handsome three-story building which was later erected about the center of Gratz Park, opposite present-day New Street.

This year the citizens were disturbed "by jockeys racing their horses through the streets." On October 21, 1793, the Town Trustees passed a law confining such racing to "the lower end of the Commons [Water Street], where stud horses can be shown."

The Rev. Stephen T. Badin, late in 1793, held the first Catholic services in the homes of Dennis McCarty, Thomas Tibbitts and others. This plan of worship continued until 1800.

Edward West, silversmith and watchmaker, built and demonstrated in 1793 a model of the first steamboat on the waters of Town Branch, dammed where the L. & N. freight depot now is located. The miniature boat moved swiftly through the water, "and cheer after cheer arose from the excited spectators."[3]

1794

In July, 1794, General Charles Scott left Kentucky with nearly 1,000 volunteers to join General Anthony Wayne in his campaign against the Indians. Their dress "was a hunting knife and leggins, with rifle, tomahawk, knife, pouch and powder horn." It was understood there was "not a drafted man in the whole command."

The first post office was established October 1, 1794, with Innes B. Brent, the first postmaster. Both the post office and jail were housed in the two-story log building at the northwest corner of Main and Broadway, which had formerly been the first courthouse.

On December 12, 1794, the Kentucky legislature chartered the Kentucky Academy, under the Transylvania Presbytery, and on February 10, 1798, granted it an endowment of 6,000 acres. It began as a grammar school, later became an academy under the Rev. James Blythe. Nearly $10,000 was raised from subscriptions in the East and on April 10, 1796, the school opened its doors. The quaint stone building of Kentucky Academy stands in the rear of the Pisgah Presbyterian Church in Woodford County.

Kentucky Academy (described above) is located about 10 miles from Lexington and still holds a place in the city's history because of its early rivalry with Transylvania. The state legislature approved a merger of the two institutions in 1798.

1795

At a meeting in the brick State House on Main Street, January 1, 1795, John Bradford, John Breckinridge, Dr. Frederick Ridgely and several other gentlemen "Resolved to organize a library called Transylvania Library." Almost a year passed before the infant library was in operation; the books were then placed in the Transylvania Seminary building.[4]

Kentucky's second newspaper, *The Kentucky Herald,* was founded February 2, 1795 in Lexington by James H. Stewart. This early news sheet survived until 1802, when John Bradford consolidated it with his *Kentucky Gazette.*

The second market house, a brick building, was erected in 1795 and occupied about two-thirds of the Public Square (Cheapside). Its back section, the Short Street end, was reserved for a "stray pen," a necessary item in the early days. This building was demolished in 1817, after a new market house had been erected the year before on another site.

A German Lutheran church was organized in Lexington about 1795; a lottery was held to purchase a lot on West High Street (site of the present First Methodist Church) between Mill and Upper streets. A story-and-a-half frame church was erected; Reverend Dishman was the pastor. The little church burned in 1815. The members, mostly German, were buried in the old graveyard in back of the church.

1796

On February 29, 1796, Lexington Lodge No. 25 (now No. 1), F. & A. M., and the trustees of Lexington held a joint lottery, each party to receive $2,500.[5] With money derived from the lottery the Masonic lodge replaced its log meeting house with a two-story brick building, completed in the fall of 1796, at the northeast corner of Walnut and Short streets. The Town Trustees put their money to an equally good use and were enabled to "sink wells, pave the streets and build bridges over the Town Fork of Elkhorn."

Rev. James Moore, in 1796, began to hold Episcopal services in a little frame church at the corner of Market and Church streets, the site of the present Christ Church.[6] This was the first organized Episcopal Church in Kentucky, although services had been held in the early 1790s on the Russell Cave farm of Capt. David Shely, near Lexington.

1797

Early in 1797, a company of gentlemen met at Postlethwait's Tavern and organized the Jockey Club — the first in Kentucky.[7] A track was built that year on a portion of what is now the Lexington Cemetery and the Forest Hill subdivision, west of the Georgetown Pike. This was the Williams Race Track, and meets were held here for the next twelve years.

John and Samuel Postlethwait, in March, 1797, purchased from Adam Steele his "elegant brick house, forty by thirty, two stories high" and containing 36 rooms. This was the beginning of Postlethwait's Tavern at the southeast corner of Main and Limestone, now known as the Phoenix Hotel. The building, erected in 1792, had been used as a school.

The Kentucky Gazette, March 15, 1797 advertised: "For Sale at public auction at 12 o'clock Wed. the 29th inst, the House adjacent to the lands of Mr. John Maxwell, lately used as a place of worship and known by the name of the Mount Zion Meeting House . . ." During the summer some members of the Mount Zion Church on South Limestone Street erected at the southeast corner of Walnut and Church streets, a frame building known as "Rankin's Meeting-House" or the "Seceesh Church," which by this time was the Associate Reformed Presbyterian Church. Thirty-six years later the building was leased to the city for use as the first public school.

The Kentucky Gazette, on May 31, 1797, carried an announcement of the first public amusement in Lexington and Central Kentucky. The notice stated that "a room for exhibition purposes has been erected" adjoining Coleman's Tavern for "an exhibition of tumbling, balancing on slack wire, slack rope walking and dancing. Admission to pit, 2 shillings; to gallery, 2 shillings and 2 pence. Doors open at sunset, performance begins at dark."

Lexington in 1797, was described as having "about 50 houses, partly frame, and hewn logs, with the chimney outside; the surrounding country was then new; a village lot could have been purchased for $30, and a good farm in the community for $5 an acre. The best farmers lived in log cabins, and wore hunting shirts and leggings."[8]

In the fall of this year, Henry Clay removed to Lexington from Virginia.

1798

On March 20, 1798, Henry Clay, who had studied law in Virginia was sworn in as a member of the bar in the two-story stone court-

Built in the late 1790s, the John Bradford house at the corner of Mill and Second played another important part in Lexington history when it was razed in 1955. The public outcry led to the formation of the Blue Grass Trust for Historic Preservation which has since become the leader in preserving historic sites.

house on Main Street. The order read: "Henry Clay, Esquire, produced in court a license, and on his motion is permitted to practice as an attorney at law in this court, and thereupon took the several oaths by law prescribed." Signed by Thomas J. Bodley, Clerk, District Court.

Lexington's population in 1798, as reported by the Town Trustees on May 9, was as follows: "Males above 12 years, 462; Females above 12 years, 307; whites under 12 years, 346; Negroes, 360." Including the county inhabitants the total population was put at 2,247 and the taxable property was listed at 189,666 pounds.

Town Trustees elected this year were William Allen, Robert Patterson, Alexander Parker, Cornelius Beatty, George Teagarden, Samuel Postlethwait and Archibald McIlvane.

By an act of the Kentucky legislature, December 22, 1798, the rival Presbyterian institutions of learning, Kentucky Academy in Woodford County, and Transylvania Seminary in Lexington, were merged under the name of Transylvania University.

1799

John Robert Shaw, the well-digger, advertised "lime for sale at Colonel Patterson's quarry at 10 cents per bushel, and he will do well-digging at 2 shillings 6 pence per foot." Shaw's autobiography, now a rare book, was published by Daniel Bradford, Lexington, 1807.

A line drawing reproduced from the 1807 book showing "the deplorable situation of John R. Shaw, late Well-Digger."

John Bradford, proprietor of the *Kentucky Gazette,* announced May 16, 1799, that he would take in payment for subscriptions: "corn, wheat, country-made linen, linsey, sugar, whiskey, ash flooring and cured hams."

This year Transylvania University established its medical college.

1800

On October 16, 1800, representatives of the five subordinate Masonic lodges in Kentucky assembled in the Masons Hall in Lexington and established the Grand Lodge of Kentucky, with William Murray, first Grand Master.[9] New numbers were given the pioneer lodges, viz: Lexington Lodge No. 1; Paris Lodge No. 2; Georgetown Lodge No. 3; Hiram Lodge (Frankfort) No. 4, and Solomon's Lodge No. 5 at Shelbyville. This was the first Grand Lodge of Freemasons established in the Ohio Valley. Charters were subsequently issued by it for subordinate lodges in Ohio, Indiana, Illinois, Missouri, Louisiana, Mississippi, Arkansas, Tennessee and Kentucky.

The Lexington Library, organized in January, 1795, as the Transylvania Library, was incorporated November 29, 1800, as the Lexington Library Association by John Bradford, James Morrison, Samuel Postlethwait and several others.[10] The collection was moved from Transylvania Seminary into quarters in the rear of Andrew McCalla's drug store on Short Street, facing Cheapside, the present site of the Herald-Leader building.

A visitor, David B. Warden, reported that "In 1800, Lexington had 1,795 inhabitants of whom 23 were Indians and 439 were slaves."

This year the Catholics in Lexington erected a small log meeting house on West Main Street, where the First Baptist Church now stands. Services were held for the next decade or so.

1801

Edward West, who had first exhibited his miniature steamboat on the waters of Town Branch in 1793, greatly improved his model and, on August 6, 1801, gave another demonstration "of a boat worked by steam, applied to oars."[11] West obtained a patent on his steamboat, July 6, 1802.

The post office was moved to the *Kentucky Gazette* office in the two-story brick State House on the south side of Main Street, between Mill and Broadway.

1802

On April 7, 1802, Transylvania University awarded its first degree, the Bachelor of Arts, to Robert R. Barr. It was the first such degree conferred in the West.

On June 30, 1802, the hated Federal excise tax on whiskey making, sales and transportation of distilled spirits was repealed. This news brought great rejoicing to many citizens of Kentucky. In the Athens of the West the Lexington Light Infantry paraded and "fired seventeen vollies of musquetry [sic], the bells rang a joyful peal, the bonfires blazed and shouts filled the air." In due time, reported the newspaper, "the citizens retired to their respective homes in perfect harmony."[12]

Gideon Shryock, ante-bellum architect, was born in this city on November 15, 1802, the son of Matthias Shryock, a local "house joiner." Gideon was the designer of Old Morrison at Transylvania University, the Kentucky State House (1827-29) at Frankfort, the courthouses of Franklin and Jefferson counties, the State Capitol at Little Rock, Ark., the Louisville Medical Academy and the Southern National Bank in Louisville. The noted architect died in Louisville, June 19, 1880, and was buried there in Cave Hill Cemetery.

Lexington's first bank, the Kentucky Insurance Company, was incorporated December 16, 1802, with permission "to issue notes payable to the bearer." It was in effect a banking house with its first location on Main Street between Mill and Broadway. It later moved into a building on Main Street between Upper and Limestone at the east corner of Boyd's Alley. The bank issued its bills

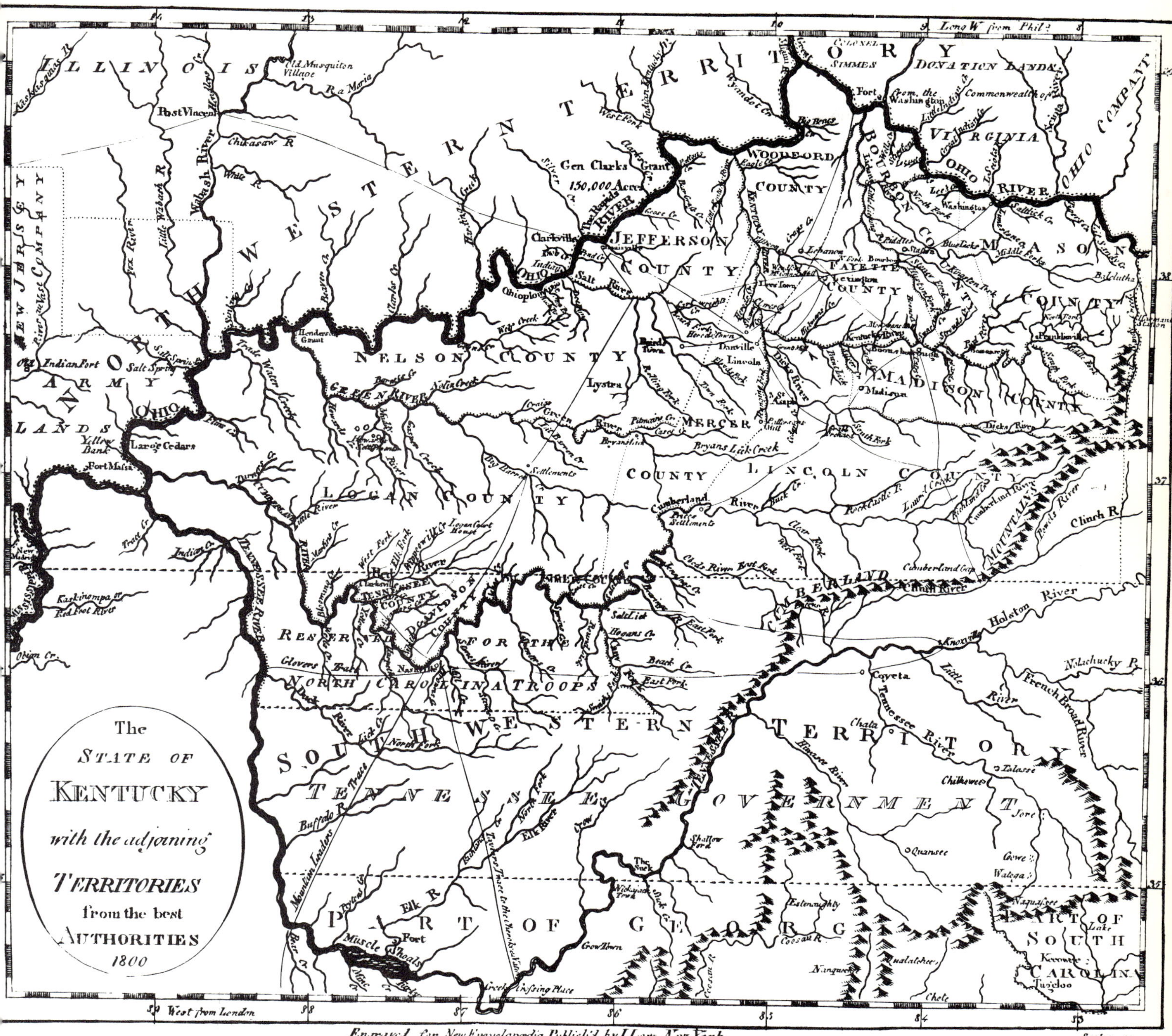

Drawn 16 years after the Filson map on page 18, this 1800 map of Kentucky begins to reflect current geography.

which circulated as currency, but failed and went out of business in the general depression of 1818.

1803

On January 31, 1803, the small stone county clerk's office in the rear of Levi Todd's residence, Ellerslie, on the Richmond Pike, burned, and with it most of the records. It was believed that "the office of Levi Todd was set on fire to destroy land records."[13] In 1818, the saved portions of the records were copied into eight volumes known as the "Burnt Records."

On August 9, 1803, John Kennedy started the first regular stage coach line in Kentucky, running from Lexington to the Olympia Springs in Bath County, by way of Winchester and Mt. Sterling. Kennedy advertised that his stage would leave the city "at four o'clock [A.M.] precisely, and will arrive at the springs the same day." Passage to the springs was 21 shillings, with 10 pounds of baggage allowed.[14]

The frame building of Christ Episcopal Church was replaced this year by a small brick church at the corner of Market and Church streets. Maddox Fisher was the general contractor.[15] The Rev. James Moore resigned as president of Transylvania University to become full-time minister of the church.

1804

Thomas Reed and John Carr, both of this city, met on "the field

A 1904 photograph of Ashland (described at the bottom of this column). Henry Clay's home was a private residence then.

of honor" near Lexington on March 14, 1804. Cause of the duel is not known. "The former was wounded in the foot, and the latter in the thigh, after passing three shots. Neither of their wounds were dangerous . . . "[16]

In June, 1804, Joshua Wilson, of "Bairdstown," purchased Postlethwait's Tavern and, after erecting a two-story brick building adjoining the old hostelry, advertised it as "equal to any in the Western Country." The new hotel fronted eighty feet on Main at the southeast corner of Limestone Street, then known as Mulberry.

1805

The central portion of Ashland, home of Henry Clay, was erected in 1805-1806; the wings were added about 1813-14 from sketches drawn by Benjamin Latrobe. Four years after Clay's death in 1852, his son James B. Clay purchased the property and demolished the old mansion which had become unsafe for habitation. It was rebuilt on the same site and with much of the same materials; Maj. Thomas Lewinski was the architect. The new structure was completed by July, 1857.[17] Ashland was sold to Kentucky (Transylvania) University in 1866, housing part of the Agricultural and Mechanical College of Kentucky. In 1882, Major Thomas C. McDowell, who married a granddaughter of Clay, purchased the property. On April 12, 1950, Ashland, owned and operated by the Henry Clay Memorial Foundation, was opened as a shrine and museum. It has been designated a National Historic Landmark.

During the period 1805-1825, Lexington was the cultural, intellectual and manufacturing center of the Western Country. It had a theater, newspaper and printing offices, a portrait painter, a sculptor, nine physicians, four silversmiths, book stores, a Masonic lodge, an Indian doctor, academies for both sexes, numerous manufactures, a three-story brick courthouse, three or four taverns, a stagecoach line, the Lexington Lyceum, a circulating library, a bank or two, and Transylvania University, which contributed most to sustain Lexington's title as the Athens of the West.

1806

On February 16, 1806, the courthouse commissioners met for the purpose "of disposing of the present courthouse (built in 1788) to the best advantage; to have a new courthouse erected on the center of the public square and to do other things they think necessary towards erecting the same."[18] Hallet M. Winslow and Luther Stevens, local "house joiners" were awarded the contract; the plans were drawn by David Sutton, an amateur architect. The three-story brick building, with cupola and spire, was completed in the fall of 1806 at a cost of $15,000. A small, two-story brick building on each side of the courthouse contained the offices of the sheriff, county surveyor, circuit and county clerks.

Lexington's first city directory was published as part of *Charless' Kentucky, Tennessee, and Ohio Almanac, for the Year 1806.* It bears the imprint of 1805, and was a frail volume of 26 pages with 10 pages devoted to the directory. Charless' work describes Lexington as having "104 Brick, 10 Stone and 187 Frame and Log houses," together with a "Court House, Jail, Market-House, and four places of public worship; an handsome lodge for Free Masons, the Transylvania University and a public library." Joseph Charless, a local printer, later moved to St. Louis and started the first newspaper in Missouri.

1807

This year the congregation of the First Presbyterian Church on North Mill Street below Short, sold its church property to Matthew Elder and the following year moved to a new site at Broadway and Second Street.

1808

William Worsley and Samuel Overton on March 12, 1808, established *The Reporter,* later styled the *Kentucky Reporter,* in Lexington. As its name implies, it stressed local news and was less concerned with foreign affairs than the *Kentucky Gazette.* In 1832 the paper merged with the *Lexington Observer.*

After the First Presbyterian Church moved from its frame building on North Mill Street, the congregation erected a handsome two-story brick church, 80 by 50 feet, with galleries around three sides. The tip of the spire was 104 feet above the ground. This fine church was located on the southwest corner of North Broadway and Second Street and was ready for occupancy in the summer of 1808. A view (drawing) of this church may be seen in *Ballou's Pictorial* magazine, Boston, May 19, 1855, in a sketch, "View of Lexington, Kentucky." This church was razed in 1857.

On October 12, 1808, the most important theatrical event in the Western Country occurred, the opening of Luke Usher's New Theater in Lexington, capable of seating 500 to 600 people.[19] The building, formerly a brewery, was remodeled by Usher into a theater at the northwest corner of High and Spring streets, and extended (downhill) to Vine and Spring streets. The Thespian Society performed the opening production — a comedy, Richard Cumberland's *The Sailor's Daughter,* and a farcical afterpiece, Coleman's *Ways and Means, or A Trip to Dover.* Usher's was the first permanent theater in the early West, although traveling shows and strolling actors had played in tents, the courthouse and in various inns and taverns for several years.

A later drawing shows the courthouse built in 1806 (described at left) and torn down in 1883.

A later portrait of Henry Clay, the master of Ashland.

Mrs. George Beck, wife of a local artist, conducted an "Academy and Boarding School for Young Ladies" in Lexington, in the large house next to the post office. A fee of $200 per annum was charged for tuition and board, with provision that "produce will be received in part payment." Extra charges included "use of orrery, globes, etc," and for "pens, ink and slate pencils, $1½ per quarter."

1809

Henry Clay and Humphrey Marshall, both members of the Kentucky legislature, had for some time been at odds over the tariff question. Clay made an unusually harsh speech against Marshall who jumped up and called Clay a liar. The two hot-headed lawmakers came to blows and Clay challenged Marshall to a duel. On January 19, 1809, the men met in Floyd County, Indiana.[20] On the first two fires both parties missed. On the third, Clay received a wound in the hip; Marshall escaped injury. In three weeks the master of Ashland was back in the House of Representatives and the duel in no way detracted from his popularity.

In 1809, the old Jockey Club was reorganized into the Lexington Jockey Club and had charge of racing at the Williams Race Track until the club faded from the picture after the fall meeting of 1823.

Notes

1. *Kentucky Gazette,* March 19, 1791.
2. *Ibid.,* April 24, 1804.
3. *Ibid.,* April 29, 1816. Recollections of John B. West, son of the inventor.
4. Staples, *History of Pioneer Lexington,* p. 127.
5. *Kentucky Gazette,* March 12, 1796.
6. Swinford and Lee, *The Great Elm Tree,* p. 10.
7. *Kentucky Gazette,* October 17, 1797.
8. Brown, *The Western Gazetteer,* p. 91.
9. Coleman, *Masonry in the Bluegrass,* pp. 44-50.
10. Staples, *History of Pioneer Lexington,* p. 158.
11. *Kentucky Gazette,* August 10, 1801.
12. *Ibid.,* July 2, 1802.
13. Draper Mss. 13CC23. Interview with Asa Farrar.
14. Coleman, *Stage-Coach Days in the Bluegrass,* p. 32-34.
15. Fisher *vs.* Warfield, Fayette Circuit Court, April 25, 1803.
16. *Kentucky Gazette & General Advertiser,* March 20, 1804.
17. *Lexington Observer & Reporter,* July 1, 1857.
18. Fayette County Court, Order Book 1, p. 343. January, 1806.
19. *Kentucky Gazette,* October 18, 1808.
20. Coleman, *Famous Kentucky Duels,* pp. 33-39.

1810-1829

Lexington Attracts National Note

As Lexington's population passed 5000, visits by President Monroe and the Marquis de Lafayette signified the wide attention the city was attracting. The War of 1812 meant Lexington men must fight, and duels too added an air of conflict to the times.

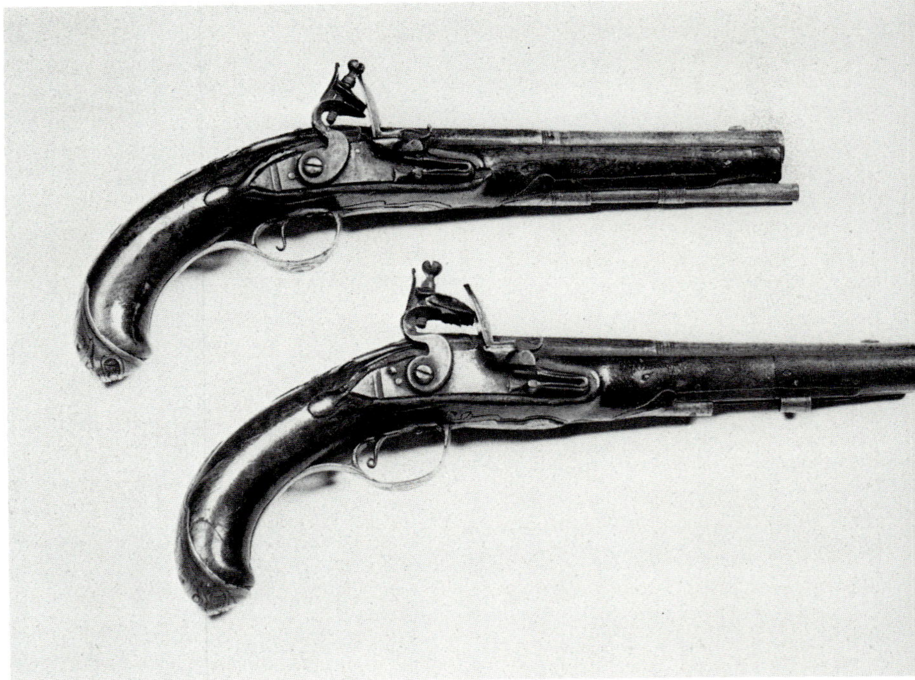

1811

Joseph Hamilton Daviess emigrated from Virginia to Danville, Ky. in 1779, and moved to Lexington in 1809. He was the first attorney from the Western Country to appear before the Supreme Court in Washington. In 1806, he prosecuted Aaron Burr. While grand master of the Grand Masonic Lodge of Kentucky, he was killed on November 7, 1811, at the Battle of Tippecanoe. An impressive funeral for the fallen hero was held in Lexington on August 27, 1812, and his remains were interred in the "old burial grounds" on West Main Street, where the First Baptist Church now stands.

1812

Captain Nathaniel G. S. Hart, a brother-in-law of Henry Clay, and Samuel E. Watson, both of Lexington, appeared on the "field of honor" January 7, 1812, in Floyd County, Indiana, opposite Louisville.[1] James McKinley and Thomas D. Owings were the seconds, respectively, for Watson and Hart. One round was fired; neither party was injured and the affair was called off.

News of the second war, the War of 1812 with Great Britain, was received in Lexington "with a brilliant illumination and great rejoicings." Six companies of volunteers were quickly raised: Hart's, McDowell's, Edmonson's, Megowan's, Hamilton's and Arnold's. A number of Lexingtonians became prominent officers: Generals John M. McCalla, William O. Butler, George Trotter, Jr. and Charles S. Todd. A rope-walk on James Erwin's Woodlands near the Richmond Pike was used as a recruiting office and barracks by the regular soldiers until the war ended.[3]

The congregation of St. Peter's Catholic Church built a small, one-story meeting house in the Catholic Cemetery on the north side of East Third Street, between the present Central Fire Station and the old Episcopal Cemetery. The new edifice was dedicated May 19, 1812, and was the first brick church erected by the Catholics in Lexington. Long known as the "old Catholic Chapel," the meeting house was razed around 1838-1839.

Daviess Lodge No. 22, F. & A. M., named in honor of Joseph Hamilton Daviess, was chartered August 29, 1812, with David Castleman, father of Gen. John B. Castleman, its first master. A number of prominent men were on its rolls, among them Cassius M. Clay, John H. Morgan, Dr. William H. Richardson, Joseph C. Breckinridge, General Leslie Combs and James G. Norwood. This lodge surrendered its charter in 1886.[2]

Matthew Kennedy, early Lexington architect, began working in this city in 1812. Among his well-known works were the handsome, three-story Transylvania University building in Gratz Park, the Grand Masonic Hall (1824-26) on West Main Street, "Grasslands" in the county, Transylvania's first Medical Hall at Church and Market streets, and his own home, a large, two-story, brick residence on North Limestone, above Sayre School. Kennedy was the first Lexington man to declare himself an architect, as distinguished from the designations of "house-joiner" and "master-builder." He is thought to have moved to Louisville shortly before his death in 1853.

1813

In May of this year, Dr. Joseph Boswell advertised that he "has procured *Genuine Cow Pox Matter,* and will innoculate a few persons every week. Any person not enabled to pay shall receive the benefit of innoculation gratis by application to him."[4]

This call-to-arms by Governor Shelby helped recruit the 4000 men that he personally led to aid Gen. William Henry Harrison in the victory at the River Thames on October 5th. The battle was the end of the hostilities in the Northwest.

1814

By November, 1814, a new and larger Episcopal church, stuccoed to resemble stone and built to accommodate 800 persons, was completed. This was on the site of the present Christ Church at Market and Church streets.[5] Matthias Shryock and Michael Gaugh were the contractors.

On November 22, 1814, a charter was issued to James Moore, Carey L. Clark and others "to open and hold a Royal Arch Chap-

TO THE

MILITIA OF KENTUCKY.

FELLOW-SOLDIERS,

YOUR government has taken measures to act effectually against the enemy in Upper Canada. Gen. Harrison, under the authority of the President of the United States, has called upon me for a strong body of troops to assist in effecting the grand objects of the campaign. The enemy in hopes to find us unprepared, has again invested Fort Meigs; but he will again be mistaken; and before you can take the field he will be driven from that post.

To comply with the requisition of Gen. Harrison, a draft might be enforced; but believing as I do, that the ardor and patriotism of my countrymen has not abated, and that they have waited with impatience a fair opportunity of avenging the blood of their butchered friends, I have appointed the 31*st day of August next, at Newport,* for a general rendezvous of KENTUCKY VOLUNTEERS. I will meet you there in person. I will lead you to the field of battle, and share with you the dangers and honors of the campaign. Our services will not be required more than sixty days after we reach head quarters.

I invite all officers, and others possessing influence, to come forward with what mounted men they can raise: each shall command the men he may bring into the field. The superior officers will be appointed by myself at the place of general rendezvous, or on our arrival at head quarters: and I shall take pleasure in acknowledging to my country the merits and public spirit of those who may be useful in collecting a force for the present emergency.

Those who have good rifles, and know how to use them will bring them along. Those who have not, will be furnished with muskets at Newport.

Fellow Citizens! Now is the time to act; and by one decisive blow, put an end to the contest in that quarter.

ISAAC SHELBY.

Frankfort, July 31*st*, 1813.

Isaac Shelby

ter under Warrant No. 1." Thus Lexington Royal Arch Chapter No. 1 was established, the first body of capitulary Masonry in the Western Country.

Saint Peter's Cemetery, or the "old Catholic Cemetery," encompassed the land around the St. Peter's Catholic Church, on East Third Street. Interments began here around 1814-1815, and continued until the Calvary Cemetery was opened on West Main Street in 1874.

1815

In January, 1815, John Darrac, a native of France, opened a school of dancing at Mrs. George Beck's Academy, where he taught "Cotillions, Hornpipes, Alemandes, German and Russian waltzes, Gavotes, Shawl Dances and Reels."[6]

Followers of the Rev. Adam Rankin erected a handsome brick meeting house, "with basement and gallery" on the east side of Market, between Church and Second streets. McChord Presbyterian Church was dedicated on July 30, 1815, with the Rev. James McChord as the first pastor.[7] On August 14, 1828, the name was changed to the Second Presbyterian Church.

1816

The Fayette Hospital was incorporated February 10, 1816, "for the accommodation of lunatics and other distempered and sick poor of Fayette County." This was the first institution of its kind west of the Alleghenies. The cornerstone of the first building, still standing on West Fourth Street and Newtown Pike, was laid on June 30, 1817. Some years later the property was taken over by the state and renamed Eastern Kentucky Lunatic Asylum. In 1867, a state grant added several new buildings and provided two hundred and fifty additional rooms.

Cincinnatus Shryock, architect and younger brother of Gideon Shryock, was born in Lexington on April 9, 1816. Among the buildings he designed were the Centenary Methodist Church, the Odd Fellows Hall (Opera House), the present First Presbyterian Church and a number of residences. He died on January 1, 1888, and is buried in the Lexington Cemetery.

A "View of the Lunatic Asylum (described above), Lexington, Ky." as included in the first (1847) edition of Collins' History of Kentucky.

Transylvania University conferred its degree of Doctor of Medicine this year on John McCullough. Although the Medical College had been in operation since 1799, McCullough was the first student to obtain that degree from a western institution.

On July 25, 1816, Lewis Sanders held a "Cattle Shew" at his farm on the Georgetown Pike, opposite Sandersville Road. Fine cattle, sheep, horses and hogs were shown. Fifteen silver cups, valued at $15 each, were awarded as prizes. Judges for this, the first fair or cattle show held in the Western Country, were Harry Innes, Fayette County; Nathanial Hart, Woodford County; Capt. John Fowler, Fayette County; Col. Hubbard Taylor, Clark County, and Capt. John (Jack) Jouett, Bath County. Another show was held here the following year, and after that the events were transferred to Fowler's Garden, off the Winchester Pike, near the city limits.

On November 23, 1816, Jeremy L. Cross, Masonic scholar and ritualist, came to Lexington and established "Lexington Council of Select Masters No. 1." The first officers were Fielding Bradford, William G. Hunt and Thomas G. Prentiss. This council, the first west of the Alleghenies, is today known as Washington Council No. 1, Royal and Select Masters.

The third market house was erected around 1815-1816 and was a long shed of frame construction, covering the entire block from Limestone to Upper, and Vine to Water streets.[8] It was razed in 1844 to make way for another market house on the same site.

1817

On February 4, 1817, the Lexington and Louisville Turnpike Road Company was organized by John W. Hunt, Charles Wilkins, Charles Humphreys and John Tilford, all of Lexington. Other stockholders and organizers were from Frankfort, Shelbyville, Middletown, Louisville and Versailles. This was the first turnpike road company in the state.[9]

On November 1, 1817, the first performance in America of a Beethoven symphony was given in Lexington under the direction of Anthony Phillip Heinrich.

Captain John Fowler opened a park adjoining Lexington in the fall of 1817.[10] The grounds extended north from Scott's Pond on the Winchester Pike (present site of Proctor & Gamble) to the federal housing (Blue Grass Park) project, former site of the

Dr. Benjamin Dudley (above left) and Dr. William H. Richardson (above), two of the city's medical pioneers, seemingly gained their notoriety in their duel (described at left below).

Kentucky Association Race Track. Fowler's Garden consisted of 50 to 75 acres and included a race track, grandstand, stables and smaller buildings. Fairs, races, livestock shows, entertainments and exhibitions of all kinds were held here. The park closed about the beginning of the Civil War.

A branch of the Bank of the United States was established in Lexington in 1817. Its first location was at the northwest corner of Mill and Church streets. It later moved to the northwest corner of Short and Market streets and continued in that location until it was forced out of business by the hostility of Andrew Jackson and the failure of Congress to renew its charter.

The brick market house on Cheapside, erected in 1795, was razed.

1818

Differences growing out of an autopsy on the body of a drunken Irishman killed on Lexington's streets, caused Dr. Benjamin W. Dudley and Dr. William H. Richardson to settle their argument with powder and ball on August 5, 1818. The two noted surgeons of the Transylvania Medical College met on the James K. Duke farm, six miles north of Lexington off the Georgetown Pike. At the word both parties fired with their flintlock pistols. Dr. Dudley stood untouched; Dr. Richardson received a serious wound in the groin which severed an artery. His life was saved by Dr. Dudley, who pressed his thumb on the large blood vessel where it passed over the ilium.[11] Eventually, the men patched up their differences and became good friends.

On April 23, 1818, John Boswell of Lexington and Charles Durand, late of New York City, faced each other with pistols in a duel "in the vicinity of this [Lexington] town." At the first fire Boswell was seriously wounded, and died the next day. Durand was slightly injured.[12]

The future wife of the 16th President was born on December 13, 1818, in a two-story brick house on the north side of West Short Street, immediately west of St. Paul's Catholic Church. This was a nine-room residence with an ell built by Robert S. Todd about 1813. In this house Todd and his wife Eliza Parker began housekeeping and here most of their seven children were born. A priests' house now occupies the site of the Todd residence.

William Worsley and Thomas Smith published the second city directory as part of their *Kentucky Almanac and Farmers' Calender for the Year 1819*. The Almanac bears the imprint of 1818, and is a pamphlet of forty-eight pages, of which the directory itself is ten pages. The title page reads: "Directory of the Town of Lexington for 1818."

Kappa Lambda, the first professional medical fraternity in America, was founded at Transylvania University by Dr. Samuel Brown, one of the faculty members.

1819

The two-story brick Masons' Hall at the northeast corner of Walnut and Short streets burned on March 19, 1819.

In March of this year fire destroyed the county jail and Luke

Megowan's Jail, the county jail, (described previous page and below) is shown in a post-Civil War photograph.

Usher's tavern, "Don't Give Up the Ship," which stood on the north side of Short Street, between Limestone and Upper streets.

Later in the year, a new county jail was erected at the northwest corner of Short and Limestone streets. Thomas B. Megowan was the jailer for many years. The building, a two-story structure of stone and brick, was demolished in 1891 and another jail (still standing) was erected at 113 East Short Street, near Limestone.

President James Monroe visited Lexington July 2 to 6, 1819, while on a tour of the country.[13] On July 3, he spoke at Transylvania University. Major William S. Dallam entertained the president, along with Gov. Isaac Shelby, Col. Richard M. Johnson, Joseph C. Breckinridge, Gen. Percival Butler, Gen. John T. Mason, William T. Barry, J. G. Trotter and other noted guests, at his home (Pope house) which stands at 326 Grosvenor Avenue. Major Dallam's dinner was on the evening of Sunday, July 4, 1819. The day before, a large banquet was given for the distinguished guests at Mrs. Keen's (Postlethwait) Tavern.

Bushrod Boswell, merchant of Lexington, and Samuel Q. Richardson, an attorney of Cincinnati, met in a duel with pistols July 23, 1819, on the Fayette-Woodford county line. Richardson's arm was broken, while Boswell "escaped his antagonist's fire." The cause of the duel was a matter of long standing.[14]

The First Baptist Church was constituted in 1817 and met for some time at Transylvania University. A house of worship was completed and opened on August 29, 1819,[15] on the west side of North Mill Street near Third, facing Gratz Park. This was a substantial two-story brick building, provided with galleries. Dr. James Fishback served as the first pastor. The last services in this meeting house were held in November, 1854.

Mount Hope, a fine two-story residence standing at 231 North Mill Street, was built around 1819 for Gen. John M. McCalla, as a standard central-hall residence. Benjamin Gratz, wealthy merchant and hemp manufacturer, acquired the property in 1824 and added the beautiful front entrance. An enlargement was added across the rear of the house in 1841 by builder John McMurtry. Mantle details in this house are especially fine. It has been in the Gratz family for seven or eight generations.

1820

On January 1, 1820, John Snow, representative of the General Grand Encampment, Knights Templar, visited Lexington and organized Webb Commandery No. 1, at the same time conferring the orders of Knighthood on eight or ten Royal Arch Masons in the Masons' Hall, at Walnut and Short streets.

The population of Lexington was counted at 5,279.

Henry Clay was master of Lexington Lodge No. 1, F. & A. M., in the first half of 1820, and grand master of the Grand Lodge of Kentucky during the latter half of the year. No other Kentucky Mason has held this high honor.

On the afternoon of March 3, 1820, the 38-room brick hotel, long known as Postlethwait's Tavern, burned. The local press said: "We hope it may soon rise like the Phoenix bird from its ashes."[16] This early "public house" was replaced with a more commodious three-story brick building which bore the name Phoenix Hotel. At the time the hostelry burned it was owned and operated by Sanford Keen.

On March 18, 1820, Dr. Lewis Marshall, of Woodford County, drew the first prize in the Grand Masonic Hall lottery which entitled him to receive the sum of $20,000. This lottery, chartered by the Kentucky legislature, authorized the Grand Lodge of Kentucky to raise "not more than $30,000 for construction of a Grand Masonic Hall in Lexington." The hall was erected several years later.

Built after the War of 1812, the John Pope House was the scene of a dinner for President Monroe (described at left).

On September 1, 1820, Madame Waldemard Mentelle, who had been a teacher at Mrs. George Beck's Academy, established "A French School for Young Ladies" in present-day (about the center) Mentelle Park, on the Richmond Pike, opposite the front gate of Henry Clay's Ashland. The charge for board, tuition and washing was $120 a year. Mary Todd, future wife of Abraham Lincoln, was a student at the Mentelle School.

This portrait of the president of the Confederacy was painted by Lexington artist William P. Welsh and hangs in Jefferson Davis Hall at Transylvania University.

David A. Sayre in 1820 opened an office as a private broker and banker. Eight years later he purchased a two-story brick residence at the northeast corner of Short and Mill streets and lived over his banking office. The firm of David A. Sayre & Company continued in business through the Civil War period and after Sayre's death in 1870 the business was continued by his nephew, Ephraim D. Sayre, until his death in October, 1889, when the bank was liquidated.[17] The Security Trust Company was the successor to David A. Sayre's bank.

1821

In July, 1821, Col. Josiah Dunham opened a girls' school, Lexington Female Academy, in a two-story brick house still standing on South Upper Street, at the south corner of Mack's Alley. The Marquis de Lafayette attended exercises at the school on May 16, 1825, and in consequence of his visit, the name was changed to the Lafayette Female Academy. Next year, the school had students from thirteen states. It continued in operation for about seven or eight years thereafter.

Jefferson Davis, the future president of the Confederate States of America, attended Transylvania University during the years 1821-1824. While in Lexington he roomed with Postmaster Joseph Ficklin at his home, which stands on the southwest corner of High and Limestone streets. Davis' brother Joseph procured a cadet's commission to West Point for him from President Monroe. After spending four years at the United States Military Academy, Davis was graduated July 12, 1828, with the brevet of second lieutenant.

A photograph from the 1940s shows the former home of Postmaster Ficklin who furnished a room for Jefferson Davis while he was a student at Transylvania (above) from 1821-24.

St. John's Chapel, a small Methodist church, erected in 1821, stood on the north side of West Main Street, . between Broadway and Spring Street, just west of the Grand Masonic Hall. Dr. Caleb W. Cloud was the founder of the church, described as "a plain, brick building, 30 feet front and 50 feet deep, having a cupola and a bell." The congregation became dissatisfied with Cloud's "ways and teachings," and the church after several years went out of existence.

1822

Church Street Methodist Church, a large, two-story brick building, erected in 1822, stood on the north side of Church Street, midway between Limestone and Upper streets. Bishop Enoch George dedicated the church, which was built at a cost of $5,000. The building was a plain, well-finished brick structure, 60 by 50 feet, with 75 pews on the first floor, and a spacious gallery on two sides and at the rear. One hundred and thirty-six years later the old church was torn down.

1823

Thomas T. Skillman in 1823, founded *The Western Luminary,* the first religious newspaper (Presbyterian) published in the Western

Country. Its purpose was "to aid in counteracting the strong infidel tendency then manifested in the city." The publisher died June 9, 1833, a victim of the cholera then raging in Lexington.

1824

The Botanical Garden of Transylvania University was incorporated January 7, 1824, with Dr. W. H. Richardson, president, and C. S. Rafinesque, secretary. Plans called for "a medical garden," park for pedestrians, a green house, museum and library.[18] About seven acres were leased from Joseph Megowan, on the south side of East Main, between Ransom Avenue (site of the Second Presbyterian Church) and Woodland Avenue. The project failed and by the summer of 1825, the garden was abandoned before any buildings were erected on it. Fifty years later Judge Speed S. Goodloe resided on the property.[19]

On the north side of West Main Street (site of H. H. Leet Co.) between Broadway and Spring street, the fine Grand Lodge Masonic Hall was erected at a cost of $35,000. Matthew Kennedy was the architect and Grand Master Asa Kentucky Lewis laid the cornerstone June 1, 1824; the hall was completed and dedicated on October 25, 1826.[20] The building was a three-story brick, with cupola and spire, and was said to have been the most pretentious building in the Western Country. Quarters on the second floor were reserved for the Grand Lodge and other rooms housed Lexington Lodge No. 1 and Daviess No. 22, as well as a Royal Arch Chapter and an "Encampment of Knights."

1825

The Marquis de Lafayette, for whom Fayette County was named, reached Louisville from Nashville on Wednesday, May 11, 1825. Accompanying the general were his son, George Washington Lafayette, his secretary Auguste Levasseur, and Bastien, his valet. The party spent the night of May 15 at the home of Major John Keen (Keeneland) on the Versailles Pike and was escorted into Lexington the next morning.[21] A number of Revolutionary soldiers gathered around Lafayette to press the hand of the last surviving major general of that war. A visit was made to Transylvania and an open air dinner was given in a grove on the Frankfort Pike after which the party attended exercises at Major Dunham's Lexington Female Academy. Henry Clay was in Washington when the "nation's guest" visited Ashland, but Mrs. Clay did the honors of his home.

That evening Lafayette was royally entertained by his Masonic brethren in the uncompleted Grand Lodge Hall on West Main Street. The supper and dancing lasted far into the night, but the elderly general retired early to his quarters at Mrs. Keen's Tavern. Next morning, Tuesday, May 17, Lafayette and his suite attended a Masonic breakfast in the large hall. The general gave a one-hour sitting to Matthew Jouett to enable the artist to complete the large portrait he had begun some weeks earlier in Washington. About mid-morning, the entourage left for Georgetown, having spent just twenty-four hours in the Athens of the West.

1826

Henry Clay, master of Ashland and secretary of state, and John Randolph, of Virginia, faced each other with pistols near Washington, D.C., on April 8, 1826. Cause of the duel was words spoken by Randolph in the U.S. Senate which Clay considered offensive and caustic. Clay and Randolph each fired without effect. On the second round Clay's shot missed, and Randolph raised his pistol, saying he would not fire on Mr. Clay again. This magnanimity brought an end to the duel.[22]

The Kentucky Association was organized July 29, 1826, "to improve the breed of horses by encouraging the sports of the turf." The first race meet was held on October 19, at the Williams Race Course, which is now a part of the Lexington Cemetery and the Forest Hill subdivision, west of the Georgetown Pike. During the years 1828-34, the company purchased 65 acres where the federal housing project is located at Fifth and Race streets. The Association constructed a mile track, grandstand, stable and small buildings. Aristides, Longfellow, Lexington, Wagner, Waverly, Ten Broeck, Grey Eagle and Glencoe ran over this track. The first grandstand with high steps was replaced in 1872,[23] and in 1889 a larger one of steel and brick was built.

1827

Matthew Harris Jouett, one of America's foremost portrait painters was born April 22, 1787, in Mercer County. He was graduated from Transylvania University in 1808, served in the War of 1812, and settled in Lexington, where he began his profession. Some of his portraits include Robert S. Todd, Judge George M. Bibb, Gen. George Trotter, Henry Clay, Asa Blanchard, Judge John Rowan, Dr. Samuel Brown, Joseph C. Breckinridge, Gov. Isaac Shelby and the Marquis de Lafayette. Jouett died on his farm near Lexington on August 10, 1827.[24]

About the year 1827, another market house was erected between Mill and Broadway, and Vine and Water streets. MacCabe described it as "a spacious brick building, 234 feet long and 42 feet wide, and contains 65 stalls." It was popularly known as the "Lower Market House," and in 1831 was leased by the Town Trustees to the Lexington and Ohio Railroad.[25] For the next three or four years this market house was used as the railroad's passenger depot and freight house.

Matthew Kennedy, Lexington's first architect, designed the Transylvania Medical Hall which was erected in 1827 at the northwest corner of Church and Market streets. This was a fairly large two-story red brick building with four pilasters across the front and blind arches along the sides. For some years the building was occupied as the medical hall and from 1842 to 1854 it served as the city hall. A fire on July 25, 1854, damaged several of the rooms, but the building itself remained intact.

In 1827, the Maysville, Washington, Paris & Lexington Turnpike Company was incorporated with a capital stock of $320,000. The 65-mile road between Lexington and Maysville was built at a cost of $426,000, including 13 toll houses and six covered bridges. It was completed in 1835.

1828

Lexington's post office was moved this year to a small, two-story brick building still standing at 307 West Short Street (north side), seventy-five feet west of Mill Street. The post office continued here from 1828 to 1855. Postmasters during this period were Joseph Ficklin, 1822-1841; Thomas S. Reed, 1841-1843; Ficklin again, 1843-1850, and Squire Bassett, 1852-1855.

1829

Charles Wickliffe, son of Robert Wickliffe, "the Old Duke," on

Built around 1820, Glendower, shown in this 1898 photograph, was the home of many noted Kentucky families including the Wickliffes and Prestons. Charles Wickliffe (below, right) died here.

March 4, 1829, published an article in the *Kentucky Reporter* denouncing Thomas R. Benning, editor of the rival *Kentucky Gazette* as a vile wretch, fiend, poltroon and slanderer. Five days later, Wickliffe visited the *Gazette* office in the old State House on Main Street, and after some "excessive quarrelling," whipped out a pistol and killed Benning.[26] Henry Clay defended young Wickliffe; the pro-slavery jury stayed out a little over five minutes and Charles Wickliffe went free.

Transylvania University's administration building, a handsome, three-story brick edifice, stood about the middle of Gratz Park, facing downtown Lexington. Matthew Kennedy designed the structure which was completed in September, 1818, at a cost of $30,000. On the night of May 9, 1829, the building was destroyed by fire. Years later, Cassius M. Clay who was a student living on the third floor at the time of the fire recalled: "My black servant stuck a tallow candle to the steps in blacking my boots — went to sleep — and the flames went like powder. I ran down with some clothes in hand and my night shirt. No one was lost, as the fire began at the top."

On October 9, 1829, George Trotter and Charles Wickliffe met to settle their differences under the code duello. Young Wickliffe had become aggrieved by a personal reference in the *Kentucky Gazette* and challenged editor Trotter. At nine o'clock the parties with their surgeons and seconds, met in the large woodland of Captain Henry Johnson, near old Donerail, off the Georgetown Pike, six miles north of Lexington.[27] At the word, both parties fired; neither bullet found its mark. On the second round Wickliffe received a mortal wound just above the hips; Trotter escaped unharmed. In a few hours Wickliffe died at Glendower, his father's residence on West Second Street. The youngest son of the "Old Duke" was buried in Howard's Grove Cemetery, seven miles out the Bryan Station Pike.

William T. Barry, noted lawyer and statesman of Lexington, was appointed postmaster general and served until 1835. A monument to him was erected on the courthouse lawn, near the present John H. Morgan statue.

Notes

1. *Lexington Reporter,* January 11, 1812.
2. Coleman, *Masonry in the Bluegrass,* p. 247.
3. Perrin, *History of Fayette County,* pp. 429-432.
4. *Kentucky Gazette,* May 15, 1813.
5. *Kentucky Reporter,* December 17, 1814.
6. *Kentucky Gazette,* January 9, 1815.
7. *Ibid.,* August 2, 1815.
8. John Lutz map of Lexington, 1835.
9. Littell's *Acts,* Vol. 5, p. 519.
10. *Kentucky Reporter,* October 1, 1817.
11. Coleman, *Famous Kentucky Duels,* pp. 43-49.
12. *The Western Monitor,* Lexington, April 25, 1818.
13. *Kentucky Reporter,* July 7, 1819.
14. *Ibid.,* July 28, 1819.
15. *Kentucky Gazette,* August 27, 1819.
16. *Lexington Public Advertiser,* March 4, 1820.
17. *Lexington Herald,* October 31, 1969.
18. *Kentucky Reporter,* November 22, 1824.
19. Ranck, *History of Lexington,* p. 304.
20. Coleman, *Masonry in the Bluegrass,* pp. 95-100.
21. *Kentucky Gazette,* May 19, 1825.
22. *National Intelligencer,* April 10, 1826.
23. *Kentucky Gazette,* April 17, 1872.
24. *Western Luminary,* Lexington, August 11, 1827.
25. Fayette County Court, Deed Book 6, p. 374, October 22, 1831.
26. *Kentucky Reporter,* March 11, 1829.
27. Coleman, *Famous Kentucky Duels,* pp. 72-85.

1830-1849

Lexington's Growth Continues

Continued growth typified by the construction of Old Morrison was slowed by two outbreaks of Asiatic cholera. Hitting in 1833 and again in 1849, the plague killed 847 Lexington citizens. Residents also came to know Cassius M. Clay the duelist, the abolitionist, and the newspaperman.

1830

The first railroad in the Western Country, the Lexington & Ohio, was incorporated by the Kentucky legislature on January 27, 1830. As planned, the road was to extend westward from Lexington "to some point on the Ohio River." On October 22, 1831, the first sill of this pioneer railroad was laid, the ceremonies being in the charge of Gen. Leslie Combs. At noon, August 15, 1832, the first car left its "moorings" at the western end of the Lower Market House with 40 passengers aboard, among them Governor Metcalfe.[1] A year later, the track was extended six miles and horse-drawn cars made regular trips with passengers and mail between Lexington and Villa Grove, a pleasure resort established by the railroad. Some months later, Thomas H. Barlow and Joseph Bruen in the latter's shop, built a locomotive but it was too small to pull the railway cars. Three locomotives, the *Daniel Boone, Logan* and *Nottaway,* were purchased in the East and put into service just prior to the road's completion to Frankfort in 1835. This year a brick passenger station was erected at Mill, Water and Vine streets. After a few years the railroad became the Lexington & Frankfort, and eventually a part of the L. & N. system.

Funeral Invitation — "Yourself and family are requested to attend the funeral of John Bradford, Esq. from his late residence [southwest corner of Mill and Second streets] at 4 o'clock, this afternoon. Monday, March 22, 1830."[2]

Giron's Confectionary, a once-famous establishment, opened in early 1815,[3] by Monsieur Mathurin Giron, stood on the west side of North Mill Street, one door below Short Street. Here, in the 1830s and 1840s the elite of the Bluegrass gathered for the fashionable Cotillion and Quadrille parties in the wide hall on the second floor. Giron boasted that he could furnish "the choicest refreshments, wines, liquors and pasty-cakes, in a style equal to any in the West." In 1844, the small Frenchman, immortalized by James Lane Allen in his *King Solomon of Kentucky,* retired from business and left Mill Street. Only the northern half of Giron's Confectionary remains; the southern part was razed in 1915.

Giron's Confectionery (described above) was followed here by a "dancing academy" operated by another Frenchwoman, M. Xaupi, in 1833. Here "waltzes, gallopades, cotillions and all fashionable modes of dancing" were taught to young Lexingtonians.

Rev. John Ward, rector of Christ Episcopal Church, established his Shelby Female Academy, later called the Young Ladies Seminary, in the Ridgely house, still standing at the southeast corner of Market and Second streets, in the early 1830s. Here Mary Todd, future wife of the 16th president, received a part of her early education. Dr. Frederick Ridgely's two-story brick house was erected around 1794-1796. Since December, 1958, the Christian Churches of Kentucky have made it their headquarters.

1832

The Hill Street Christian Church stood at 229-232 West High Street, the oldest church building in Lexington. The two-story brick building, one door east of the Asbury M. E. Church, was formerly a cotton factory; it was enlarged and remodeled into a meeting house. Here on January 1, 1832, the adherents of Barton W. Stone (Stoneites) and the followers of Alexander Campbell (Campbellites) united to form the present-day Christian Church (Disciples of Christ). Ten years later the congregation moved to the new and larger Main Street Christian Church. This historic church on High Street was razed in November, 1969, as part of the Urban Renewal Plan.

On January 12, 1832, Lexington was incorporated as a city, with Charlton Hunt as the first mayor. The city was divided into four wards, a municipal seal was adopted, the first board of councilmen was inducted into office, a workhouse was established, and the general machinery of a new government set in motion.

In March, 1832, the *Kentucky Reporter* and the *Lexington Observer* merged to become the *Lexington Observer & Reporter,* a leading newspaper in central Kentucky which continued for a number of years. In politics it was Whig and supported Henry Clay. After the Civil War, it became a staunch Democratic organ edited by Col. W. C. P. Breckinridge.

In May, 1832, Robert S. Todd purchased the fine Georgian house which stands at 574 West Main Street and moved there with his family. His third daughter, Mary Ann Todd, spent seven years of her youth and early womanhood here before going to Springfield, Illinois, where she married Abraham Lincoln. Lincoln visited several times in this house and in November, 1847, spent nearly a month while en route to Washington, D.C. No other house in Kentucky has as many associations with President Lincoln as does this brick house on West Main Street. The Commonwealth of Kentucky plans to acquire and restore it.

On September 29, 1832, President Andrew Jackson, a candidate for reelection, visited Lexington for the second time.[4] A grand barbecue was given in his honor at Fowler's Garden, off the Winchester Pike at the city limits. On Sunday, September 30, the president attended services in the First Presbyterian Church and the next day he and his entourage left the city by horseback.

1833

On April 1, 1833, the Associate Reformed Presbyterian Church leased to the City of Lexington its church building which the Rev. Adam Rankin had built some years before. The old meeting house stood at the southeast corner of Walnut and Short streets. In 1834, the first public school in Lexington was begun here, with Joseph Gayle, principal.

This 16-room brick mansion, The Meadows, was a central part of many of the activities of this period. The Gideon Shryock-designed house (see page 94) was the scene of the marriage of Mary Jane Warfield to Cassius M. Clay in February, 1833.

On the north side of East Third Street, several hundred yards east of Walnut, is located the old Episcopal burial ground which was opened in the spring of 1833, just before the cholera plague struck the city. Charlton Hunt and his wife deeded the four-acre plot to the trustees of the Christ Episcopal Church on December 31, 1832. Here are buried, in addition to a number of cholera victims, John Postlethwait; John Grimes, portrait painter, Franklin Combs, son of Gen. Leslie Combs, Matthias Shryock; James O'Bannon, and Mrs. Eunice Lockwood who was killed in a stagecoach accident. John McMurtry designed the quaint, brick sexton's cottage standing about the middle of the grounds.

On June 3, 1833, the Asiatic cholera came to Lexington. The pestilence increased and during the next three or four weeks 1,500 people were sick and, at the peak of the epidemic, were dying at the rate of fifty to sixty a day. Business houses were closed, grass grew in the principal streets and all who could fled the city. There remained only a few to care for the sick and stricken. William "King" Solomon, a town vagrant, remained and faithfully dug graves and buried the dead. By the middle of July, the plague subsided, leaving 502 deaths in the city.

The Lexington Orphan Asylum was founded in 1833 to care for children whose parents died in the cholera plague. For many years it was housed in a two-story brick building on West Third Street at the entrance of the present Hampton Court. For the last 30 or 40 years the home has been located at 511 West Short Street, in the "Widow Parker" house, just west of the priests' house of St. Paul Church.

1834

On June 24, 1834, the Episcopal Theological Seminary of Kentucky was chartered and established in Lexington. A large, two-story brick house, still standing at 437 West Second Street, was purchased[5] for the school which had its first commencement on November 9, 1834, with two graduates. Bishop Benjamin B. Smith and the Rev. Henry Caswell served as teachers. With only six students, the trustees voted in May, 1841, to dissolve the seminary. In 1951, the school was revived and located at the rear of the Church of the Good Shepherd at East Main Street and Bell

Court. Currently there are five or six instructors with thirty students in the seminary.

The Bank of Kentucky was established in Lexington in 1834 and conducted a successful business in the city until it closed its doors on March 13, 1865, at which time the residuary interests were purchased by the private banking house of David A. Sayre & Company. For the years 1838-39, Robert S. Todd was president and William Waller and Thomas H. Pindell, cashiers.

St. Catherine's Academy, a Catholic school for girls, on the east side of North Limestone adjoining St. Peter's Church, was moved to Lexington in 1834, from St. Francis Church at White Sulphur in Scott County, where it had been organized four years before. Sister Ann Spalding was the first mother superior. St. Catherine's Academy became the Lexington Catholic High School in 1952, and remained until 1958, when the site was purchased by the City of Lexington. The building, which had been erected in 1847, was razed in 1959.

Morrison Chapel, better known as Old Morrison, a handsome Greek revival building on the Transylvania University campus, was designed by Lexington architect Gideon Shryock, and dedicated on November 4, 1833, although not completed at that time. The years 1831-34 were devoted to building the structure at a cost of $38,000, which was provided from a bequest of Col. James Morrison of Lexington. Lexington's first (1833) cholera plague delayed construction of the three-story building, with a massive two-story Doric portico and six fluted columns, approached by a broad flight of steps. Today it is the oldest building on the campus.

1835

On January 25, 1835, "a painful and heart-rendering accident" occurred on the Lexington & Ohio Railroad, as the train returned from Villa Grove, six miles west of the city.[6] The "burden car," in which a number of men were standing, was thrown off the track as the train rounded a curve; several were thrown under the car wheels. Mr. Lewis Lonkard was instantly killed and two or three men suffered broken legs and several others were severely injured. Earlier that morning, a ten-year-old Negro slave boy, in attempting to jump on the "locomotive engine," fell beneath it and was crushed to death.

The Northern Bank of Kentucky was organized in February, 1835, and opened for business in June of that year. It purchased from the Bank of the United States its branch house in Lexington at Market and Short streets, its debts and specie, and was appointed to wind up the affairs of the Lexington branch. It conducted a very extensive and successful business until its liquidation in 1889. Its capital was, for those days, the stupendous sum of $1,800,000, and it conducted branches at Paris, Barbourville and Covington. The bank had its headquarters in a two-story brick building at the northwest corner of Market and Short streets.

On August 21, 1835, Richard Clayton, in his *Star of the West* balloon, ascended from a field near the western edge of Lexington. This balloon ascension, the first in Kentucky, reached a height estimated by Clayton at two miles as it passed over the village of Athens. Something went wrong with the gas valve, causing the "aerial bark" to make a rapid descent to earth, landing about 15 miles from Lexington on the Thomas A. Jones farm in Clark County. Clayton escaped unharmed, but his balloon was severely damaged.[7]

Old Morrison.

Lexington's most famous citizen, Henry Clay, was using this private "traveling coach" presented to him by admiring friends from New Jersey in 1833 as he traveled overland between "Ashland" and the nation's capitol. The coach is now at Ashland.

John Lutz's map of Lexington for 1835 shows the following roads leading out of the city: Hickman (Nicholasville); Henry's Mill (Newtown); Russell's (Russell Cave); Curd's (Harrodsburg); Tates Creek; Georgetown; Limestone (Paris); Strode's (Winchester); Frankfort, and Leestown leading to the town of that name above Frankfort on the Kentucky River. "Smith's Waggon Road," from Lexington to Limestone (Maysville), as shown on earlier maps, was the first route from the Ohio River to Lexington and Central Kentucky.

Edward P. Johnson, the stagecoach king of the thirties, forties and fifties, lived at "Johnson's Grove," on the site of Sayre School on North Limestone Street opposite Second. Edward P. Johnson & Company, with offices in the Phoenix Hotel, had stagecoach lines operating over Kentucky to Louisville, Maysville, Cincinnati, and extending as far south as Bean Station, Tennessee. Johnson's lines tapped the Cumberland Road (U.S. 40) at Zanesville, Ohio, and carried the U.S. mail south from Maysville, through Paris and Lexington, to Florence, Alabama.

In November, 1835, a handsome granite shaft, ten feet tall and enclosed with a plain iron fence, was erected on the courthouse lawn (site of the Morgan statue) to the memory of William T. Barry, noted lawyer, statesman, U.S. senator and postmaster general under President Jackson. He died while en route to Spain to assume the position of minister and envoy. After the fourth courthouse burned in May, 1897, Barry's cenotaph was broken up and used in the foundation of the Harrison city school on the west side of Bruce Street, near Second.

1836

On the evening of August 29, 1836, fire was discovered in the Grand Masonic Hall on West Main Street. The local fire engines, *Kentuckian, Resolution* and *Lyon* were soon on the scene, but the fire was beyond control and by midnight the hall was in total ruins.[8] After the building had been erected, the Grand Lodge was unable to pay Dr. Lewis Marshall the money ($20,000) he had won in a lottery, and had mortgaged the property to him. On November 4, 1835, he had foreclosed on his claim, and was the owner of the building when it burned.

1837

On June 14, 1837, the first lodge of Odd Fellows was established here; it was Friendship Lodge No. 5. This lodge ceased to operate after 1870.

Father Edward McMahon raised $5,000 and built St. Peter's Catholic Church, with columns and pilasters, on the east side of North Limestone, several hundred feet south of Third Street. John McMurtry designed the brick edifice, which was formally dedicated on December 3, 1837. Lightning struck the tower on May 31, 1890, and burned it down to the bell section.

St. Peter's Roman Catholic Church (described above) is shown in a 1929 photograph. The view of the church which stood on North Limestone is taken looking toward the northwest corner of the building. The church had been replaced by a new St. Peter's on Barr Street that same year and was demolished in the fall of 1930.

1838

In April, 1838, the Lexington Athenaeum was established in one room of a building on Jordan's Row, opposite the courthouse. Here foreign and domestic newspapers and magazines were provided for the members' perusal.

In August, 1838, a great railroad festival was held in Lexington to raise money for the proposed Louisville, Cincinnati & Charleston Railroad, which was designed to link the Bluegrass with the South and West. Lack of public interest caused this ante-bellum railroad enterprise to be abandoned and no trackage was ever laid.

Asa Blanchard, Kentucky's leading silversmith, operated in Lexington for about 30 years, beginning in 1808. In 1816, he advertised that he kept on hand "patent lever watches" and had "a supply of silver coffee pots, sugar dishes, pitchers, etc." Blanchard was especially noted for his fine coin silver soup ladles and mint julep cups. He died here on September 15, 1838.[9]

Julius P. Bolivar MacCabe published in book form his *Directory of the City of Lexington and County of Fayette for 1838 & '39*. The thin volume of 136 pages, bound in boards, contains the first printed history of Lexington; in addition there are listed the city inhabitants and a record of the land owners in Fayette County with their acreage.

1838 Private Schools — The Young Ladies Seminary, 52 North Mill Street, Rev. John Ward, principal, with 61 pupils; Lexington Female Academy, 18 Market Street, Samuel D. McCullough, principal, 40 to 50 pupils; and the Lexington Female Seminary, 7 East Main Street, with 25 to 30 pupils.

Several private road companies operated out of the city in 1838-39; viz: Lexington & Winchester Turnpike Company, Richard Chiles, president; Lexington, Versailles & Frankfort Turnpike Company, Eben Milton, president; Danville, Lancaster & Nicholasville Turnpike Company, T. S. Proctor, president; Lexington, Harrodsburg & Perryville Turnpike Company, C. M. Cunnington, president; Lexington, Georgetown & Covington Turnpike Company, Roger Quarles, president; Lexington & Richmond Turnpike Company, James Shelby, president, and Maysville, Washington & Lexington Turnpike Company, John Armstrong, president.

1840

The Masonic Grand Lodge (described above right).

On July 3, 1840, the cornerstone of a second Masonic Grand Lodge Hall was laid at the northeast corner of Walnut and Short streets. The handsome, three-story brick building was dedicated on September 1, 1841. It was the design of Prof. C. R. Preziminski of Transylvania University and cost around $25,000. During the Civil War the building was taken over by the Federal Army and used as a hospital, prison and recruiting office. After the Grand Lodge moved to Louisville, the hall which had become greatly dilapidated, was sold at auction for $10,000 on May 21, 1887, and was demolished in February, 1892.[10] Central Christian Church now occupies the site.

During the 1840s and 1850s and for some years earlier, the Kentucky Colonization Society, with headquarters in Lexington was transporting freed slaves to its colony in Liberia. During its existence, 1829-1859, the Society sent a total of 658 emigrants, or slightly less than 22 per annum, to "Kentucky in Liberia," on the west coast of Africa. After thirty years of trials and privations, the whole scheme, which Henry Clay had advocated as both "practical and logical," proved to be little more than a fantastic dream.

During the two or three decades prior to the Civil War there were several silversmiths in Lexington who made beautiful coin silver cups, ladles, goblets and flatware. Among these skilled craftsmen were Asa Blanchard, Eli C. Garner, Samuel Ayres, J. Best, E. F. Winchester, William P. Poindexter, David A. Sayre and John Byrnes.

1841

Duelists Cassius M. Clay and Robert Wickliffe, Jr., both of Lexington, met on the "field of honor" May 5, 1841, on Col. John Croghan's Locust Grove plantation near Louisville. Col. William R. McKee was Clay's second and his surgeon was Dr. Alexander Marshall; Wickliffe's second was Gen. Albert Sidney Johnston, with Dr. Charles Caldwell acting as his surgeon. Pistols at thirty feet (10 paces) were used. Two rounds were fired, but nobody was injured and friends of the parties adjusted the difficulty.[11]

Temple Chapter No. 19, Royal Arch Masons, was chartered in Lexington on September 1, 1841, and continued to operate until October 20, 1874, at which time its charter was surrendered to the Grand Chapter.

The erection of the large Hill Street Methodist Church on the south side of High Street between Upper and Mill streets was begun in 1841 and finished the next year. The church was dedicated for divine service by Bishop Henry B. Bascomb, who in 1842 was appointed president of Transylvania University. This church became the Methodist Episcopal Church South after 1845, and adhered to the southern faction of the denomination. The building was razed in 1907 and the present First United Methodist Church was built on the site at 214 West High Street.

1842

Main Street Christian Church, a commodious building completed in 1842, stood on Main Street at the site of the Union Station, just west of the Harrison Avenue Viaduct. It was a large, two-story brick building with tower, and had a seating capacity (with balcony) of 800 persons. In 1870, the congregation divided into two factions; one group forming the Broadway Christian Church, and the other moved (in 1894) to the new Central Christian

Main Street Christian Church (described below).

Church at Walnut and Short streets. After the turn of the century the old church was given over to plays, shows and other public gatherings; it was razed during September and October, 1903.[12]

1843

On February 23, 1843, the trustees of the First and Second Presbyterian Churches purchased eight acres of ground for a burial site.[13] Known as "Waverly Square," the cemetery covered the entire block between Limestone and Upper, and Sixth and Seventh streets. Many prominent families were buried here, but after the mid-1880s, the old cemetery was little used and finally abandoned. On September 11, 1890, the churches sold the cemetery ground for $8,000 to Thomas T. Skillman, Richard H. Courtney and Joseph M. Scott. The bodies were removed and more than 375 were reinterred in the Lexington Cemetery.

In May, 1843, Eliza, a young woman only one-sixty-fourth African, was sold as a slave at public auction on Cheapside. Calvin Fairbank, noted anti-slavery worker, bid her in for $1,485 with money supplied by prominent out-of-state abolitionists.[14] When the crowd heard that the Rev. Mr. Fairbank was buying Eliza to free her, "a great shout went up." After receiving her "free papers," Eliza moved to Ohio, married and lived for many years.

Early in August, 1843, a "desperate recounter" occurred between Cassius M. Clay and Samuel M. Brown at a political rally at Russell Cave, six miles north of Lexington on the Russell Cave Pike. As young Robert Wickliffe was speaking, Clay challenged one of his statements and was delivered a heavy blow by Brown. Said the local press: "In the affray, Mr. Clay was shot by Mr. Brown, the ball striking him just under the last rib on the left side, but coming in contact with the scabbard of Mr. Clay's bowie knife, did no injury. Mr. Brown was badly cut in several places about the head and face by Mr. Clay with the knife."[15] Henry Clay defended his cousin "Cash" and won an acquittal; he kept clear his record of never having lost a criminal case in the last thirty years of his practice.

In the Main Street Christian Church, the Rev. Alexander Campbell, of Bethany, Virginia, debated the Rev. Nathan L. Rice, of Paris, Kentucky, on the subject of "Christian Baptism." Henry Clay acted as moderator, assisted by Judge George Robertson and Col. Speed Smith. The historic debate, which ran from November 15 through December 2, 1843, was published in book form (912 pages) by A. T. Skillman, Lexington, 1844.

1844

The Lexington Theater was located on the south side of West Short Street, opposite "Grandma Parker's" house in a large brick building which was one of the largest in the West. The theater opened on April 2, 1844, but did not prosper and several years later went out of business.

During the spring of 1844, a new and larger market house of frame construction was erected on the site of the previous one. Commonly known as the Upper Market House, it covered the block, from Limestone to Upper, and from Vine to Water streets. It was principally a long shed, with a series of wagon stalls which opened on both Water and Vine streets. Farmers backed their wagons into these stalls and sold their produce from their carts, much as was done at Louisville's Haymarket. This building was demolished in 1879 to make way for the sixth market house (Jackson Hall) built on the site.

Miss Delia Webster, a New England schoolteacher, and the Rev. Calvin Fairbank, "agents" of the Underground Railroad, secretly conducted three Negro slaves from Lexington to Maysville and started them on their way to Canada. On September 28, 1844, the couple was tried in Lexington for their abolition activities. Fairbank drew a 15-year sentence in the State Penitentiary; Miss Webster received a two-year term. She was later pardoned by Governor Crittenden, but continued her anti-slavery activities in Trimble County until she was run out of the state by irate slaveholders.

The True American *office (described next page).*

1845

Cassius M. Clay's anti-slavery newspaper, *The True American,* made its appearance on the streets of Lexington on June 3, 1845, with the motto: "God and Liberty" at its masthead. This modest, four-page news sheet was received in the slaveholding Bluegrass with bitter scorn and contempt. Threats were made on Clay's life and for the suppression of the paper. On August 11, 1845, while Clay lay ill, a mob armed with a bogus court order seized the printing plant, dismantled the presses and shipped them out of the state. Clay later secured a judgment of $2,500 in the Jessamine Circuit Court against the "committee of sixty" which had wrecked his printing plant, at No. 6 North Mill Street. The two-story brick building which housed *The True American* was torn down around the turn of the century.

1846

On Saturday afternoon, January 10, 1846, Lafayette Shelby, grandson of Kentucky's first governor, shot and killed Henry M. Horine in front of the Phoenix Hotel, where both had attended a drinking party.[16] Shelby's trial began on July 1, 1846, with Henry Clay as senior counsel for the accused. Due to the large crowds in attendance, the trial was moved to Old Morrison at Transylvania University. Clay succeeded in dividing the jury and bringing about a mistrial. A wave of indignation spread among the citizens when Shelby was let out on $10,000 bail. During the night of July 12, a group of enraged citizens stretched a rope between two large trees on the courthouse lawn facing Main Street, and from it were hung life-sized effigies of Judge Richard A. Buckner, Jr., and the eight jurors who had voted to acquit the prisoner. Next morning the effigies were taken down and paraded around town to the tune of the "Rogue's March," winding up on Cheapside where they were publicly burnt amid the shouts and hoots of a wild and excited crowd. Young Shelby, who had escaped conviction, fled to far-off Texas and was heard from no more.

On May 11, 1846, a call was made for 50,000 Mexican War volunteers. Two local companies, commanded by Captains Cassius M. Clay and Oliver H. P. Beard, were attached to Col. Humphrey Marshall's regiment.[17] Before leaving Lexington on June 4, the soldiers assembled at Old Morrison and were addressed by Professor B. H. McCown. Each man was then presented with a Bible. On July 4, 1846, they embarked on the steamer *Bunker Hill* at Louisville en route to Memphis, and marched overland to Little Rock and through Texas to Camargo on the Rio Grande where they entered Mexico.

1847

The cornerstone of the new Christ Episcopal Church at the northeast corner of Church and Market streets, was laid March 17, 1847. Major Thomas Lewinski designed the building, which was erected on the site of the old church built in 1814. The new meeting house was completed in May, 1848, at a cost of $20,000.[18] Today it is the oldest church building in Lexington.

The Rev. Edward F. Berkley baptized his good friend Henry Clay in the parlor of Ashland on June 22, 1847, in the presence of a few close friends. The water was applied by hand from a cut-glass urn, which had been given to Clay by a manufacturer of such wares in Philadelphia. Thus, at the age of seventy, the master of Ashland, who long professed an interest in the Episcopal Church, became a member through baptism and a month later received the rite of confirmation at the hands of Bishop Benjamin B. Smith in Morrison Chapel.

Noted Lexington artist William P. Welsh painted this Henry Clay portrait to hang in Henry Clay Hall at Transylvania.

Devotion Lodge No. 160, F. & A. M., was chartered September 2, 1847, with Oliver C. Anderson, the first master. This is the second oldest Masonic lodge in the city with a membership of about six hundred.

Second Presbyterian Church stood on the east side of Market Street, between Church and Second streets. It was designed by Major Thomas Lewinski; John McMurtry was the builder. The handsome structure with a tower was erected in 1846-1847, and dedicated on October 31, 1847. It had a seating capacity of over 700. A large iron plaque over the front entrance read: "Presbyterian Church, Erected A.D. 1846. Holiness to the Lord." This

church stood on the site of the McChord Church, built in 1815.

1848

A telegraph line between Lexington and Louisville was established this year, and the first message was transmitted over the wires on March 6.

On August 5, 1848, Lexington and Fayette County were thrown into the greatest excitement when it was learned that 75 slaves, armed and desperate, had escaped from their masters and were on the verge of insurrection. A reward of $5,000 was immediately offered for their capture. Captain Oliver H. Beard, of Lexington, with a large company of volunteers headed for Cynthiana on August 8. Most of the runaway slaves were captured in a large hemp field near the Bracken County line; three from Fayette County, thought to have been the ringleaders, were tried and hanged.[19]

1849

By an act of the legislature, on February 5, 1848, the Lexington Cemetery was organized at 833 West Main Street. In the spring of 1849, the 40-acre woodland of Thomas E. Boswell was acquired and the Rev. Robert J. Breckinridge dedicated the new cemetery on June 25, 1850. John McMurtry, local architect, designed the gatehouse which was erected during 1849-50; it was replaced with the present one built in 1890. The cemetery's holdings today amount to 110 acres under development, with an additional 60 acres held in reserve. Approximately 45,000 persons have been buried in the cemetery since the first interment of Robert S. Boyd, on October 2, 1849.

During June and July, 1849, the dreaded cholera again visited Lexington. While the mortality was great, it was not comparable to the 1833 attack. Out West Main Street, the newly opened Lexington Cemetery received the remains of 283 citizens. A total of 345 persons lost their lives in this second outbreak.

The Kentucky Statesman, a long-time Democratic newspaper in Lexington, was established October 7, 1849, by a company of businessmen, with B. B. Taylor its first editor. During the Civil War, the paper was suppressed by the military in September, 1861. The first issue of the *Kentucky Statesman* after the war appeared on January 1, 1867, with William C. Goodloe and W. Owsley Goodloe as editors and proprietors. *The Statesman* was a favorite news sheet in Central Kentucky for many years.

Rev. Adam Rankin's old meeting house at the southeast corner of Walnut and Short streets was demolished, and a fine two-story brick building, known as Morton School No. 1 was erected on the site. This school building was a duplicate of Harrison School No. 2 erected the same year and still standing at 614 West Main Street. Classes were discontinued here in 1902 or 1903, when a new Harrison School on Bruce Street near Second was completed.

Old Lexington City School (described above).

Notes

1. *Lexington Observer & Reporter,* August 16, 1832.
2. Duff Collection, Lexington Public Library.
3. *Kentucky Gazette,* January 2, 1815.
4. *Argus of Western America,* Frankfort, September 26, 1832.
5. Fayette County Court, Deed Book 10, p. 96, April 17, 1834.
6. *Lexington Observer & Reporter,* January 26, 1835.
7. *Frankfort Commonwealth,* August 29, 1835.
8. *Kentucky Gazette,* September 1, 1836.
9. *Ibid.,* September 20, 1838.
10. *Lexington Morning Transcript,* February 28, 1892.
11. *Western Citizen,* Paris, May 21, 1841.
12. *Lexington Morning Herald,* September 27, 1903.
13. Fayette County Court, Deed Book 27, p. 130. February, 1843.
14. Coleman, *Slavery Times in Kentucky,* pp. 132-134.
15. *Lexington Observer & Reporter,* August 5, 1843.
16. *Ibid.,* January 14, 1846.
17. Ranck, *History of Lexington,* pp. 353.
18. *Lexington Observer & Reporter,* May 24, 1848.
19. Coleman, *Slavery Times in Kentucky,* pp. 89-91.

1850-1869

Expansion, Then — The War!

The exploding expansion of the railroads in the first decade of this period represented the commercial development that seemingly could not be stopped. The death of Henry Clay might have been a sign of dark days ahead, but until the War Between the States pitted Kentuckians against one another, the unrivaled expansion of the Athens of the West continued.

1850

Melodeon Hall, a three-story, iron-front building still standing at the southwest corner of Main and Upper streets, was the opera house during the years from 1848 to 1887. A large auditorium, capable of seating from 300 to 400 people was on the second floor, with a balcony running around the third floor. General Tom Thumb, the 28-inch "giant" appeared here on January 28-30, 1850. Numerous shows, plays and concerts, as well as public gatherings were held in the opera house, which had its principal entrance on Main Street. Another opera house (Odd Fellows Hall) at Main and Broadway was also in use part of the time Melodeon Hall was occupied.

The Maxwell Spring Company was chartered November 30, 1850, by the Kentucky legislature and purchased 25 acres of land for a park south of the present McLean Stadium on the University of Kentucky campus. This acreage included the well known Maxwell Spring which was located in the valley between the stadium and the Patterson Office Tower. A grandstand, a speaker's stand and several buildings were erected. Maxwell Spring was the time-honored gathering place to celebrate the Fourth of July and hold militia musters and drills and other public celebrations. Here also on occasion, Henry Clay, Robert J. Breckinridge, Cassius M. Clay, William T. Barry and many others addressed immense crowds.

On December 7, 1850, the Kentucky Agricultural & Mechanical Association was incorporated in Lexington and purchased a number of acres south of the Maxwell Spring Company's acreage between Limestone and Rose (Van Pelt) streets.[1] Benjamin Gratz was president; Henry C. Payne, vice-president; David A. Sayre, Henry T. Duncan and seven other men, directors. The association's purpose was to hold annual fairs, exhibitions of all kinds, "cattle shews," running and trotting races, to show purebred livestock and thoroughbred horses, and to display agricultural and farming implements.

At Bryan Station Pike and Castlewood Drive stands Loudoun, a fine example of the Gothic Revival style of Kentucky architecture, erected in 1849-50 by Francis K. Hunt. New York architect Alexander J. Davis prepared the plans and John McMurtry erected the building, which at the time was considered the largest and finest house in Kentucky. Total cost of the structure was $30,300. Col. William Cassius Goodloe, U.S. minister to Belgium, lived here. Since 1930 the historic house and grounds have been the Castlewood city park.

This 1873 photograph shows John McMurtry, the well-known architect of the period and his son Pat Isaac.

The Kentucky Central Railroad was the outgrowth of the Maysville & Lexington and the Covington & Lexington railroads, both of which constructed a line south to Paris during the early 1850s. On July 8, 1875, the Kentucky Central was organized and took over the Covington & Lexington and leased the Maysville & Lexington Railroad. Its passenger depot in Lexington was at the west end of Short Street, near Payne and Dodge streets in the valley east of the Lexington Cemetery. On September 22, 1891, the Louisville & Nashville acquired ownership of the Kentucky Central Railroad.

The African Methodist Church was built on Vine Street in the rear of the present Kentucky Central Building (Lafayette Hotel) and near the Harrison Avenue Viaduct. It was torn down many years ago and it stood on part of the ground of the Bryan-Hunt building, recently demolished. This church was a large brick building with a square front above the eaves of the main entrance.

Porter Clay, younger brother of Henry Clay, was a Lexington cabinetmaker, lawyer, and Baptist minister. In 1815, he was appointed auditor of the state, and in the late 1840s moved to Camden, Arkansas where he died (1850) and is buried.

1851

On March 22, 1851, the City of Lexington subscribed to $200,000 in stock of the proposed Lexington & Danville Railroad. It later acquired the Cincinnati, Lexington & East Tennessee Railroad from Lexington to Nicholasville, which David Sinton had built during the years 1855-56. To cross the gorge of the Kentucky River, John A. Roebling, designed a huge suspension bridge to be supported by a tall stone tower at each end. Due to the unsettled times and financial causes, construction was stopped on the road, leaving the towers in place. Completed parts of the Lexington & Danville Railroad were acquired in April, 1874, by the Cincinnati Southern Railroad and incorporated in its system. The stone towers were removed in 1929.

At 341 Madison Place stands Botherum, a charming house more Roman than Greek, which was erected in 1851 for Madison C. Johnson, brother-in-law of Cassius M. Clay of Madison County. John McMurtry was the designer of Botherum, which in its early days fronted on West High Street. Major Johnson was the prototype for Colonel Romulus Fields, one of the principal characters in James Lane Allen's book *Two Gentlemen of Kentucky.* For many years Botherum was the home of James A. Todd, son of Dr. Lyman B. Todd, Lexington's Civil War postmaster and first cousin of Mrs. Abraham Lincoln.

Lewis C. Robards, Lexington's leading slave dealer, acquired the old Lexington Theater in 1851 and advertised that "his new Negro jail, formerly the theater, on [West] Short Street, is now finished and ready for use." Robards occupied the property for some years and several other slave dealers followed him until the beginning of the Civil War.

1852

The Lexington & Big Sandy Railroad was incorporated in January, 1852, with a view toward building a railroad from Ashland to Lexington. Between 1854 and 1857, twelve miles of the roadbed were constructed from Ashland to Coalton. However, the plan was stopped by the 1857 panic and by 1860 the project was abandoned, with little trackage having been laid.

As the Lexington & Ohio Railroad did not go farther than Frankfort, it later came to be known as the Lexington & Frankfort Railroad. The Louisville & Frankfort Railroad was started eastward some eight or ten years later. It was not until the spring of 1852, with the completion of a bridge over the Kentucky River and a tunnel under the Frankfort hill, that through rail service was established between the Derby City and the Bluegrass Capital.[2]

Thomas White and Benjamin Johnson, both of this city, met on the dueling grounds of the James K. Duke farm near Donerail at 5 P.M., on October 5, 1852. Double barreled shotguns were used, each loaded with a single ball, distance 40 yards. "At the first fire, White fell, the ball of his antagonist passing through his brain and killing him instantly." Johnson was not injured. Both men were students of Transylvania University.[3]

At 320 Linden Walk stands the Gothic Revival house Elley Villa, built by John McMurtry for William R. Elley in the early 1850s. The property passed to John L. Barclay and then to Judge William C. Goodloe who became owner of the house in the 1860s. Soon after his death in 1870, it was bought by Gen. William T. Withers. In 1877, the St. Joseph Hospital was established here by two Sisters of Charity, who operated the institution until 1878. Oliver P. Alford, uncle of Lieutenant Governor Mitchell Alford, came to Lexington in 1885 and purchased the property and renamed it Aylesford. It is currently occupied as a private residence.[4]

Botherum (described at left).

Reception of the Remains of

HON. HENRY CLAY.

THE YOUNG MEN OF

LOUISVILLE,

(irrespective of party,) are requested to meet at the COURT HOUSE, this evening, at 8 o'clock, for the purpose of making arrangements to receive the Remains of Mr. CLAY, and to escort them to Ashland. It is hoped that every young man in the City will attend.

July 6, 1852.

Henry Clay died in Washington, D.C., June 29, 1852, aged 75 years. His body was taken on a grand tour by steamboat and train and covered 800 miles. The long trip from the nation's capital back to Lexington was the grandest display of funeral pageantry the country had ever known. Clay's funeral was held on July 10, 1852 and 30,000 people witnessed the ceremonies. His remains were interred in the family plot in the Lexington Cemetery until a suitable monument could be erected to his memory.

1853

At the May term, 1853, of the Fayette Circuit Court, Abraham Lincoln was sued by members of Oldham, Todd & Company for $472.54, alleged to have been for "money collected for said firm and unaccounted for."[5] Lincoln voluntarily assumed the burden of proof, took the depositions of persons whose accounts he was charged with having collected, and by them disproved the charge. The surviving partners, Oldham and Hemingway, were forced to dismiss the suit and pay the court costs. The firm located at Sandersville, near Lexington, manufactured woolen and cloth goods.

In July, 1853, the Kentucky Agricultural & Mechanical Association obtained provisional use of the Maxwell Spring Company's grounds. A large two-story amphitheater was built capable of seating 800 persons, together with a brick floral hall, several cottages and 150 stables. A race course was laid out. This became the Fair Grounds where the annual fairs and exhibitions were held and races run. Today this acreage is the central part of the University of Kentucky campus.

The city was first lighted with gas on the night of Wednesday, July 27, 1853, and hard-oil lamps went out of use. Several brick buildings (one still standing) were erected by the Lexington Gas Company at the southeast corner of West Main and Patterson streets, opposite the First Baptist Church. This project for the manufacture of artificial gas for street illumination was completed by the firm of John Jeffrey & Company, of New York, and was the first of its kind west of the Allegheny Mountains. During the period 1902-1934, the brick buildings were used as a freight depot for the interurban car system.

1854

The Lexington & Frankfort Railroad freight depot was completed in May, 1854, on West Vine Street near Patterson. It was described as "a most substantial brick building on a stone foundation, upwards of 300 feet in length and about 85 feet wide." The building was razed in 1915, and the present L. & N. freight depot was erected on the site.

Rev. London Ferrill, a noted Negro preacher, died on October 12, 1854.[6] He had been born a slave in Virginia and came to Lexington as a young man. Ferrill was reported to have "baptised upwards of 5,000 persons," as pastor of the First Baptist Church. He was buried in the old Episcopal Cemetery on East Third Street.

William "King" Solomon, hero of the 1833 cholera plague, died on October 23, 1854, aged 79 years. The *Kentucky Statesman* said: "He heroically devoted himself to digging graves for the victims of the scourge, while almost all others, under the influence of panic, had deserted."[7] Cholera was spread by contaminated drinking water, but Solomon supposedly quenched his thirst only with whiskey and thus did not get the cholera. He was buried in the Lexington Cemetery where, on September 18, 1908, a handsome marker was erected over his grave, with the quotation from James Lane Allen's short story: "For had he not a royal heart."

On November 1, 1854, David Sayre purchased a large, two-story brick house at the northeast corner of Mill and Church streets, and established the Transylvania Female Seminary. On October 1, 1855, the school, renamed the Sayre Female Institute, was moved to the Edward P. Johnson mansion on North Limestone opposite Second Street. Through the years many boys and girls have attended the school, which in 1954 celebrated its 100th anniversary. Currently, instruction is given through the high school grades.

1855

On January 23, 1855, Misses Ellen and Louisa Jackson purchased the large, three-story brick building (afterwards the Britling Apartments) at 343 South Broadway[8] from John McMurtry and opened a fashionable girls' school known as the Jackson Female Seminary. The sisters sold the property at the outbreak of the Civil War and returned to Virginia.

Theophilus Steel, a medical student at Transylvania University, and James Blackburn, a law student of the same school, met with pistols on February 16, 1855, near Moreland's Tavern in Bourbon County. On the first fire, Blackburn was shot in the thigh, receiving a slight wound. They shook hands, "and the parties returned to the city as friends."[9]

This spring the Lexington Post Office was moved from 307 West Short Street, to a large, three-story brick building at the northeast corner of Limestone and Main streets. The Post Office continued here until 1861. Both buildings are still standing. Jesse Woodruff was postmaster during this period.

Judge George "Old Buster" Robertson published his *Scrap Book on Law and Politics, Men and Times,* A. W. Elder, printer, 402 pages, Lexington.

First Baptist Church, a "plain two-story brick with beautiful windows," was begun on April 1, 1853, and formally dedicated August 19, 1855.[10]It was erected at a cost of $15,000 on the east side of North Mill Street between the present First Presbyterian Church and Church Street. Sparks from a burning livery stable across the street set the church on fire and destroyed it on the night of January 3, 1859.

1856

Merrick Lodge No. 31, Independent Order of Odd Fellows, was established in Lexington on March 3, 1856. Its large hall at Main and Broadway was destroyed by fire in 1886, and its five-story brick building at Limestone and Short burned in 1917. The lodge currently meets in its hall at 1108 Winchester Pike.

Cincinnatus Shryock was the architect for the large, three-story brick Odd Fellows Hall, at the southeast corner of Main Street and Broadway. The building was completed in December, 1856, with a seating capacity of 1,200 to 1,500 persons. The opera house occupied the second floor, with an entrance from Main Street. Many important meetings, shows and gatherings were held here in the late ante-bellum days and Civil War period. Several lodges of Odd Fellows and Masons held their meetings in this building, which resembled a Gothic church minus a spire.

The Odd Fellows Hall (described above) was also the Opera House. It was built in 1856 at a cost of $40,000 and was destroyed by fire on January 15, 1886.

The Henry Clay monument (described below).

1857

Early in 1857, a group from the Hill (High) Street Methodist Church purchased the 30-year-old Transylvania Medical Hall at the northwest corner of Market and Church streets. Here they established Morris Chapel which was dedicated on Sunday, January 18, 1857.[11] After eight or nine years the church was discontinued. In 1866, the building was sold to the city for a public library, which had its quarters here until early into the twentieth century. In later years, the old building housed the Jennie Hanson magazine agency, the YMCA and the University Club. The historic structure was demolished in March, 1954, to make way for a parking lot opposite Christ Church.

The First Presbyterian Church, built in 1808, at the southwest corner of Broadway and Second streets, having become greatly dilapidated, was torn down and another brick building erected on the site. The new church was dedicated May 17, 1857,[12] and five days later the General Assembly of the Presbyterian Church convened here. The congregation worshipped in this church until 1870.

On July 4, 1857, the cornerstone of the imposing memorial to Henry Clay was laid, and the monument was dedicated on July 4, 1861. Stone for the monument in the Lexington Cemetery came from Grimes' quarry on Boone Creek in Fayette County. Julius W. Adams was the designer, Major Thomas Lewinski was resident engineer, and the contractor was John Haly of Frankfort. The total cost of the monument including the 14-foot statue of Clay atop the shaft amounted to $58,000. Funds were privately raised by the Clay Monument Association, which built the memorial. Lightning hit the statue twice, on July 23, 1903, shattering Clay's head, and again on September 10, 1910, tearing off the right hand and thigh.

On the evening of July 9, 1857, thirteen men gathered in the Lyon Fire Engine House at 149 South Limestone and organized the *Lexington Rifles,* a social, military company. Officers elected were John Hunt Morgan, captain; Major Thomas Lewinski, commandant; Charles H. Britton, first lieutenant; J. H. Shropshire, second lieutenant; J. R. Gross, third lieutenant, and R. Cox, ensign. Dues were set at $20 per annum. Regular meetings and drills were held until April 16, 1861, when the unit disbanded. Morgan and most of the *Rifles* joined the Confederate Army.

1858

On July 10, 1858, William Barker, killed Joseph Beard, the city marshal. An angry mob stormed the jail, overpowered the turnkey and dragged Barker from his cell. He was rushed to the old brick courthouse and hanged from a large beam shoved out a second-story window, facing Cheapside. After hanging for nearly four hours in the bright July sun, Barker's body was cut down by Captain Perry Beard, half-brother of the slain official.[13]

Slave traders multiplied in Lexington to such an extent that by the end of 1858 there were as many slave dealers as there were mule traders. Among the more prominent were Lewis C. Robards; Bolton, Dickens & Company; Robert H. Thompson & Company; Griffin & Pullum; Blackwell, Murphy & Thompson; A. B. Colwell; P. N. Brent; R. W. Lucas; Silas and George Marshall; Northcutt, Marshall & Company; W. F. White & Company; William F. Talbott and John Mattingly.[14] There were also numerous smaller traders in and around Lexington, less prosperous than some of the above mentioned, who engaged in buying and selling slaves.

1859

Captain Ben C. Blincoe, jailer during the Beard-Barker case of 1858, was murdered at his front door May 27, 1859, by a man named Alexander Warren from Madison County, who disemboweled him with a Bowie knife. Said the local paper: "It required the protection of the sheriff and the *Lexington Rifles* to prevent a mob action similar to the one the previous year." Blincoe's marker in the Lexington Cemetery reads: "Capt. B. C. Blincoe. Born 19 Feb. 1809. Died 27 May 1859."

Harper's Weekly's *drawing of the hanging of William Barker (above).*

This view, made from a faded glass negative, shows a slave sale on Cheapside, the public square and trading place.

The Ashland Rifles, the third military company in the city, in order of time, was organized in 1859. Officers elected were: Robert J. Breckinridge, Jr., captain; B. R. Allen, first lieutenant; T. M. Frazier, second lieutenant; C. W. Fouschee, third lieutenant; C. S. Randall, first sergeant. The Ashland Rifles were mostly southern in sympathy, and furnished only three recruits to the Federal Army in the Civil War.

In the spring of this year, C. S. Williams published the fourth city directory of Lexington, titled: *Lexington Directory, City Guide, and Business Mirror,* in a hard-back volume of 124 pages, plus 72 pages of Post Office directory. The book was printed by Hitchcock & Searles, Lexington.

1860

After their church on North Mill Street burned in 1859, the congregation of the First Baptist Church erected a new church on the old Baptist "burying grounds" on West Main Street, just west of Felix Street and opposite Patterson Street. The church fronted on Short Street and was dedicated January 1, 1860. The Rev. William H. Felix was called as pastor. Early in the Civil War the church was used as a hospital for sick and wounded soldiers. It burned in 1863.

One of the noted military companies raised in this city was the Lexington Chasseurs, organized May 9, 1860, in the grand jury room of the old brick courthouse. Officers elected were: Sanders D. Bruce, captain; J. C. Cochran, first lieutenant; W. F. Matheny, second lieutenant; C. H. Harney, third lieutenant; Dr. T. J. Bush, surgeon, and C. H. Brutton, color bearer. With the outbreak of the Civil War, the company went mainly into the Union Army.[15]

During the 1860-1870 period there were several banks doing business in Lexington: Agricultural Deposit Bank; Grinstead & Bradley; Lexington City National Bank; Branch Bank of Kentucky; First National Bank; Northern Bank of Kentucky; Tilford & Barclay; David A. Sayre & Company; J. M. Hocker & Company, and Proctor & Hocker.

In 1860, the city's population was estimated to be 9,321.

1861

A large meeting to honor the Lexington Light Infantry was held in the Odd Fellows Hall at Main and Broadway, on the evening of January 18, 1861, when a handsome flag was presented to the company. Old soldiers of the War of 1812 were escorted to prominent seats on the stage. A roll call of the captains of the Lexington Old Infantry, from 1789 to 1861, was read by Judge Levi L. Todd. Music was furnished by the Newport U.S. Band under the direction of Lieut. P. T. Swaine. Members of this company went mostly into the Union Army at the outbreak of the Civil War, with Samuel W. Price as captain.

Early in April, 1861, excited groups of citizens gathered on Cheapside, on Jordan's Row, in hotel lobbies and in the shadows of the old brick courthouse discussing divergent views on the attack on Fort Sumter. Outside the telegraph office at Mill and Short streets anxious men awaited the outcome of the attack. Some rejoiced at the fall of Fort Sumter; others received the news with indignation and regret. Nowhere were the sentiments more mixed than in Lexington. Family ties were rent asunder; father against son and brother against brother.

Toward the end of May, 1861, the six military companies of the Bluegrass, which had become a part of the State Guard — the Lexington Rifles, the Lexington Old Infantry, the Governor's Guard, the Flat Rock Grays, the Lexington Chasseurs and the Bourbon Rangers — went into Camp Buckner[16] at the Fair Grounds, under the command of Col. Roger Hanson. With "their glittering bayonets, floating flags and martial music" they presented the citizens of Lexington with their first real view of the war.

Lexington's Civil War Post Office was located in a three-story brick building at the southwest corner of Mill and Short streets and remained here through 1874. Dr. Lyman B. Todd, first cousin of Mary Todd Lincoln, served two terms as postmaster from 1861 to 1869.

Dr. Lyman Todd in a picture made around 1900. He was at the deathbed of President Abraham Lincoln in Washington, D.C.

Late in the summer of 1861, Federal forces took over the Fair Grounds of the Kentucky Agricultural & Mechanical Association on South Limestone Street for military purposes. Here hundreds of blue-clad soldiers camped and drilled. On the evening of December 18, 1861, the large amphitheater was destroyed by fire, along with the brick floral hall and the other buildings. After the war, the annual fairs for some years were held across town on the grounds of the Kentucky Association Race Track, where the Federal Housing Project, Fifth and Race streets, is located.

Several "public houses" were in operation in Lexington during the Civil War years 1861-1865, viz: Brent House, east side Limestone, near Short; Broadway Hotel, northwest corner Short and Broadway; City Hotel, southwest corner Vine and Limestone; Curd House, south side Vine, between Upper and Mill; Fayette House, corner Short and Limestone; Megowan Hotel, north side Short, between Upper and Limestone, and the well-known Phoenix Hotel, at the southeast corner of Main and Limestone.

1862

Although Lexington was occupied by Federal forces during most of the Civil War, it was repeatedly threatened by the Confederates. After General Edmond Kirby Smith defeated the Union troops at the battle of Richmond, August 30, 1862, he moved on to Lexington, September 2, with his 11,000 gray-clad veterans.[17] On the 18th of September, 1862, a Confederate Thanksgiving day was observed in the city and gratitude was expressed for "the recent victories which have crowned the Southern arms." Not less than a million dollars worth of property and arms enough for ten thousand men fell into the hands of the Confederates, counting the supplies captured at Richmond and those taken at Lexington. The Confederate troops left Lexington on October 8 and retreated to Tennessee.

At daybreak on October 18, 1862, the Union forces encamped at Henry Clay's home were completely taken by surprise as Gen. John Hunt Morgan and his hard-riding cavalry suddenly appeared and, dashing through the woods at Ashland, "poured in a most deadly volley of musketry and grape on all sides." About 500 men with their arms and equipment were captured by the Confederates. "The whole force was either killed or captured," reported *The Vidette,* "and a company was sent into the city to disperse about a hundred of the enemy who had taken refuge in the courthouse. This was quietly done, the whole of them surrendering after firing a few shots. At the request of friends we made no arrests, and left the city as quiet as we found it and pursued our march to Versailles."[18]

HEADQUARTERS

Department, No. 2,

LEXINGTON, OCTOBER 3d, 1862.

GENERAL ORDERS No. 132.

The General Commanding had hoped that the Currency of the Confederate States would have been taken at its par value, and that no effort would be made to depreciate it. He regrets to find that he has been disappointed, and that the Order heretofore issued has been misunderstood. Confederate Money has been refused by some, and by others exorbitant rates have been demanded.

The payment by the Government for supplies in Confederate money carries with it the obligation to protect its circulation. All efforts to discredit it must cease.

To avoid any further misunderstanding, it is ordered that the currency of the Confederate States be taken at its par value in all transactions whatever, public or private.

The refusal to take it, or the exaction of exorbitant rates, will be treated as a military offence, and punished accordingly.

By command of Gen. BRAXTON BRAGG.

GEORGE WM. BRENT,
Chief of Staff & A. A. G.

While the "Battle of Lexington" was in progress, a detachment of Morgan's men captured a large American flag from a small body of Union soldiers in camp at the Fair Grounds, and after walking on it, proceeded to drag it through the streets of the city. Miss Ella Bishop, a young lady of seventeen, wrested the flag from the Confederates and, wrapping it around her body, made off with it saying she would give it up only with her life. When the Union troops arrived back in town a few days later, Brigadier General G. Clay Smith named the encampment — Camp Ella Bishop — "in honor of the courageous girl whose exhibition of high spirit closely parallels that of Barbara Freitchie."

After John H. Morgan's capture of the Union forces at Ashland, Fort Clay was erected on a commanding eminence overlooking the city near the Versailles Pike.[19] It was a quadrangular earthwork, surrounded by a ditch with magazine, well and drawbridge, and was on the site of the present Clay-Wachs Stock Yards.

1863

Roger W. Hanson was born in Clark County on August 27, 1827, and practiced law in Winchester and Lexington. In a duel in 1848 with William Duke he was wounded in the right thigh. During the Civil War, Hanson espoused the southern cause, going on the staff of Gen. John C. Breckinridge. He rose to the rank of brigadier general and, as commander of the Orphan Brigade (the First Kentucky), was severely wounded at the Battle of Stone River on January 2, 1863, and died two days later. His remains were interred in 1866 in the Lexington Cemetery where a handsome monument was erected by the surviving members of his brigade.

On the morning of May 23, 1863, the large three-story Medical Hall of Transylvania University at the northwest corner of Broadway and Second streets, was destroyed by fire. The building, designed by John McMurtry, had been completed in October, 1840, at a cost of $23,915.[20] The hall, in addition to a big amphitheater, contained several lecture rooms, a medical library, an anatomical museum and faculty rooms. At the time of the fire, the building was full of sick and wounded Federal soldiers under the care of Dr. Robert Peter.

Grinstead & Bradley's Bank was established in 1863, with offices on Upper Street, between Main and Short in Jordan's Row. After the death of Bradley in 1883, the bank was under the charge of James A. Grinstead for several years, and after his death (Oct. 9, 1886), the business wound up in a cloud of lawsuits.

Mrs. Leslie Carter, famous stage actress, was born as Caroline Louise Dudley, in Lexington, on June 10, 1863, in a large, two-story stone house which stood on West Main Street east of the Lexington Cemetery.

Thomas H. Barlow, inventor, was born in 1791 in Nicholas County. In 1826, he constructed a small locomotive, the first in the Western Country. Barlow also invented a planetarium, which

In 1866, this building was converted into the Lexington Library after having served as Transylvania's Medical Hall, City Hall, and a Methodist church. It was razed in 1954.

showed the movements of the sun, moon, earth and the planets. Copies of this instrument were purchased by the United States Military and Naval academies, the Universities of Nashville and Mississippi, and Sayre Institute. With his son Milton, he invented in 1855 a rifled cannon and a machine for rotting hemp by steam. He died in June, 1863, and was buried in the Cave Hill Cemetery in Louisville.

1864

"You and your family are respectfully invited to attend the funeral of Mrs. Lucretia Clay, relict of the Hon. Henry Clay, from the residence of her son, John M. Clay, tomorrow (Friday) afternoon, the 8th inst, at 4 o'clock. Carriages will be waiting on Cheapside at 3 o'clock. Lexington, April 7, 1864."[21]

Oliver Frazer, another of the early Lexington portrait painters, was born in Fayette County on February 4, 1808. Frazer studied for several months under Matthew H. Jouett and, in 1828 went to Philadelphia to become a pupil of the great Thomas Sully. Returning to Lexington, the young artist did portraits of Mr. and Mrs. Henry Clay, Jr., Waller Bullock Redd, Robert Frazer, Richard H. Menefee, Thomas H. Shelby, Gov. Isaac Shelby, Col. William R. McKee, Matthew T. Scott, Edward M. LeGrand and others. Frazer died at Eothen (Malvern Hill) on the Georgetown Pike on April 9, 1864. He is buried in the Lexington Cemetery.

Henry Clay was born April 12, 1777, in Hanover County, Virginia and, after studying law under Chancellor George Wythe, migrated to Lexington in November, 1797. He married Lucretia Hart and by this union there were eleven children — five sons and six daughters. Henry, Jr., was killed at Buena Vista (Mexican War) in 1847; James B., died in Canada in 1864; Theodore W., died in 1870 and Thomas H., in 1871. John M. Clay survived until 1887. All of Clay's daughters died before his death in 1852. On April 8, 1864, the body of Henry Clay was removed from his family lot and placed in the newly completed Clay monument[22] in the Lexington Cemetery. At the same time, the remains of Mrs. Clay, who had died April 7, were deposited near her husband; they repose in marble sarcophagi in the vaulted chamber.

Gen. John Hunt Morgan, CSA, was born in Huntsville, Ala., on June 1, 1825, and moved to Lexington with his parents four years later. He was engaged in hemp manufacturing and other businesses and in 1857 organized the Lexington Rifles. Morgan entered the Confederate service in August, 1861; was captured near Lisbon, Ohio, July 26, 1863, and confined in the Columbus, Ohio penitentiary. He escaped on November 27, 1863, and was killed at Greenville, Tenn., on September 4, 1864. Morgan's remains were first buried in the Sinking Spring Cemetery, Abington, Virginia, and a week later were taken to Richmond, Virginia, and buried with full military honors in the Confederate plot. After the war his body was returned to Lexington and interred in the Lexington Cemetery on April 17, 1868.

On June 8, 1864, Brig. Gen. John H. Morgan met and routed Generals Burbridge and Hobson at Mt. Sterling and pressed on to Lexington. Morgan's men, tired, hungry and badly needing supplies, raided most of the Lexington stores, helping themselves to whatever they needed, and took $10,000 from the Branch Bank of Kentucky. The Confederate raiders gladly "exchanged" their jaded mounts for fresh thoroughbred horses. John M. Clay alone lost $25,000 in horseflesh, besides his fine sorrel mare Skedaddle, for which he had been offered $8,000. By mid-afternoon that day Morgan and his men rode out of town toward Cynthiana, West Liberty and over the mountains into Virginia.

Bolton, Dickens & Company's slave jail on West Short Street, formerly known as "Robards' Negro jail," was taken over by Federal forces at the beginning of the Civil War. The theater-jail was

John Hunt Morgan, "the Thunderbolt of the Confederacy."

being used as a military prison when it burned on the evening of July 13, 1864.[23] The building was said to have had 250,000 bricks in its walls, which were advertised for sale after the fire. Some years later, in 1893, the First Congregational Church was built on the site.

In 1864 C. S. Williams published the fifth city directory under the title: *Williams' Lexington City Directory, for 1864-5* in a hardback volume of 122 pages, plus 106 pages of Post Office directory. The imprint shows Lexington, Ky. 1864. The publisher complained that numerous men, fearing they were being listed for the draft, "indignantly denied us the information which we sought."

1865

Joseph H. Bush, noted Lexington portrait painter, was born in 1794, probably in Mercer County, Ky. From 1814 to 1817, young Bush studied art in Philadelphia and spent his time in Louisville and in Lexington, where he had a studio on the second floor of David Sayre's bank, corner of Mill and Short streets. Some of his better-known works include portraits of Gov. James Garrard, Gen. William Clark, Maj. William Preston, Gen. George Rogers Clark, Richard Pindell, Judge John Speed, Gen. Zachary Taylor, Dr. Benjamin W. Dudley and a self-portrait. The Kentucky artist died at his brother's home in Lexington on January 11, 1865.

On February 22, 1865, the Agricultural & Mechanical College of Kentucky was established through the Morrill Land Grant College Act, which provided that the new school be located "in the county of Fayette, in or near the city of Lexington." The newly-chartered college was made a part of Kentucky (Transylvania) University, retaining however, a certain independent status. Early in 1866, John Bowman, regent, purchased the Henry Clay mansion and farm for $85,000. In addition, for some $40,000 he acquired the farm Woodlands, the estate of James Erwin, son-in-law of Henry Clay. Together these tracts comprised 433 acres for the new college, which opened in 1866, with a dozen instructors and about 200 students. Classes were held at Ashland and at Woodlands. In 1869, Dr. James K. Patterson became the presiding officer of the A. & M. College, which continued to hold classes on the two campuses until February, 1882, when it moved to the present University of Kentucky campus, formerly the Fair Grounds.

On February 28, 1865, an act of the legislature provided for the consolidation of Transylvania University, with Kentucky University at Harrodsburg, which John B. Bowman had built upon the ruins of Bacon College. Transylvania, the oldest college in the West, had fallen on lean years and, as the buildings of the Mercer County institution had burned the year before, the trustees of Kentucky University moved their assets to Lexington and absorbed the older school. The enlarged university began operations on October 2, 1865, "under the most flattering auspicies," and was known as Kentucky University until 1908.

News of General Lee's surrender at Appomattox Courthouse, Virginia, on April 9, 1865, was received in Lexington by the "loyal" citizens with cheers, ringing of bells and thundering salutes from Fort Clay. Demonstrations followed far into the night with "fire works, gun fire and a great illumination." It was a day of rejoicing for many, but of overwhelming sorrow for the friends of the South, who remained off the streets and in their homes. The Civil War was over and slavery belonged to history.

This post-Civil War photograph shows the south side of Main Street between Broadway and Mill Street. The firm at right, DeLong & Co., distributed the planter advertised in the ad on page 56.

The First National Bank was formed in Lexington in the spring of 1865, and is today known as the First Security National Bank & Trust Company. The present bank has been formed by the merger, acquisition or consolidation of fourteen banks.

The Lexington City National Bank was chartered this year, with William C. Goodloe, president, and A. M. Barnes, cashier. This was the second bank organized in Lexington under the National Banking Act of 1863.

First Baptist Church was erected on West Main Street, facing on Short Street, after the previous one burned. The church was a commodious brick structure, erected at a cost of $20,000. It was dedicated on August 20, 1865, only to be destroyed by fire on February 3, 1867. It was believed that the fire, the third suffered by the congregation, was started by workmen repairing the tin roof.

In 1865, the College of the Bible began in Lexington as a school of Kentucky (Transylvania) University, with Robert Milligan, its first president. In 1878, a charter was obtained by the school and it continued to meet in Old Morrison until 1895, when it built on the campus a large, three-story brick building with tower, facing Broadway.[24] In the spring of 1950, the College of the Bible moved to a new campus across town on South Limestone Street, opposite the University of Kentucky. On the school's 100th anniversary in 1965, its name was changed to the Lexington Theological Seminary, its present designation.

After the close of the Civil War, Professor Samuel G. Mullins conducted a well-known school in the building where the Jackson Sisters had their female seminary at 343 South Broadway. Robinson Institute was in operation during the years 1865-1867, and was succeeded by the Baptist Female College in 1868.

1866

After the close of the Civil War, H. Howard Gratz revived the *Kentucky Gazette* (established 1787), and issued the first copy on June 23, 1866. The paper continued to run until 1910.

Another of Lexington's century-old business concerns is the Kaufman-Straus Clothing Company which began operations in the summer of 1866, at what was then 58 East Main Street. This firm which was known as the "One Price Clothing House," specialized in men's and boys' clothing. The business is currently located at 135 West Main Street and recently has been known as the Kaufman Clothing Company.

On August 29, 1866, Oceola Tribe No. 8, Improved Order of Red Men, was organized on the third floor of Viley & Company's drug store, with James Chrystal, sachem. After meeting for a number of years in Kastle's Hall on Main Street, between Mill and Broadway, the lodge went out of business.

In September, 1866, the Rev. Silas Totten started the Christ Church Seminary which was described as "a church boarding and day school for girls" in the John McCauley house at the southwest corner of Lexington Avenue and East Maxwell Street. The house had been built in 1851 with John McMurtry as architect. In 1875, the school was headed by Rev. J. S. Shipman, rector of Christ Church, with Miss Helen Totten as principal. The Seminary continued to 1884. Around 1900, Professor A. N. Gordon opened his "Gordon School for Boys" in the old McCauley residence. Currently, and for some years back, the building has been occupied as a private residence, and the Maxwell Street Presbyterian Church, erected in 1916, stands in its front yard.

Thomas Hunt Morgan, son of Charlton Morgan and nephew of Confederate General John Hunt Morgan, was born on September 25, 1866, in the Hunt-Morgan House, Second and Mill streets. He received his B.S. and M.S. degrees from the Agricultural & Mechanical College of Kentucky, and Johns Hopkins awarded him the Ph.D. degree in 1890. Dr. Morgan in 1933 won the Nobel Prize for discoveries concerning the laws of heredity, the only Kentuckian ever to win this high honor. He also was awarded honorary degrees from a number of American and European universities. He lived for many years in Pasadena, California, and died there December 4, 1945.[25]

1867

The Order of Good Templars, a temperance society, was organized in Lexington with the establishment of Arlington Lodge on November 22, 1867. Next year on December 8, Ashland Lodge of the same order was established; both lodges met for a number of years in the Kastle Building on the north side of Main Street between Mill and Broadway.

Lexington's sixth city directory was published by Alexander Maydwell, Jr., titled: *Maydwell's Lexington City Directory for 1867,* in a hardback book of 166 pages, printed by Miami Printing and Publishing Co., Cincinnati.

1868

On the second Monday in February, 1868, Professor A. S. Worrell opened a "female school under the patronage of the Baptist denomination,"[26] at 343-47 South Broadway (site of the Britling Apartments). He was succeeded by the Rev. J. C. Freeman. In 1872, the Baptist Female Seminary, also known as the Lexington Female College, was in a flourishing condition under the Rev. Dr. Robert Ryland, of Richmond, Va. His son, Professor William S. Ryland, assumed control of the school late in 1877; it continued to operate until about September, 1888.

First Baptist Church, another large brick Baptist church, was erected on West Short Street, west of Felix Street. Said the local press: "The First Baptist Church was dedicated on Sunday last [July 5, 1868]. Rev. Dr. Woolfolk preached the dedicatory sermon

An 1869 grocery circular.

Lexington, Ky., July 10, 1869.

We continue to issue our Circulars, and think that all parties will be benefited by an examination of our goods. Everything that we offer is first-class—we deal only in articles of the best quality—and solicit your patronage.

SUGARS.

N. O. Brown,	Crushed,
Yl-de-fonso Brown,	Powdered,
Demarara,	Granulated,
Coffee, A,	Cut Loaf.

COFFEE.

Java,	Ceylon,
Mocha,	Rio.
Brazilian,	

TEAS.

Imperial,	Young Hyson,
Oolong,	Japan.

MEATS.

Potted Meats, Ham,	Strasburg Meats,
" " Tongue,	Country Bacon,
" " Yarmouth Herring,	Broiling Beef,
" " Beef,	Dried Tongues,
" " Anchovy Paste	Devilled Ham,
	" Tongue,
	" Turkey,
Sugar Cured Hams,	" Lobster.

FISH.

Roe Herring (Potomac),	Oysters, spiced & pickl'd
Herring (Dried),	Oysters (Cove),
Shad (Potomac),	Anchovies,
Neat Herring, in ½ bbls.	Sardines,
Salmon (Fresh),	Boneless Sardines.
Codfish (Desiccated),	

FRUITS.

Prunes,	Pears [Canned],
Dundee Marmalade,	Plums [Canned],
Almonds,	Green Gages [Canned],
Raisins [Layer],	Dried Cherries,
" [Valencia],	"Petit Pois" [French],
" [Sultana],	Cocoanut [Desiccated],
Citron,	Capers,
French Olives,	Currants,
Spanish Olives,	Guava Jelly,
Olives [Stuffed],	Canton Ginger,
Sugar Tamarinds,	Ginger Preserves,
Corn [Winslow's],	Champignons,
Peaches [Canned],	Essences of all kinds.
Pineapple [Canned],	

CRACKERS.

Aêrated,	Fruit Biscuit [Import'd]
Boston,	Albert " "
Butter,	Pearl " "
Soda,	Nic Nac " "
Oyster,	A B C " "
Ginger Snap,	Mixed " "
Foerster's Crackers,	Picnic,
Graham's Biscuit,	Water,
Farina,	All kinds of Kennedy's
Milk,	choice Crackers.

SOAP OF ALL KINDS.

PICKELS AND SAUCES.

English Pickles,	Worcestershire Sauce,
Castleman "	Pepper "
Olive Oil,	Continental "
Essence of Anchovies,	Cumberland "
Mushroom Catsup,	London Club "
Walnut "	Cabinet "
Tomato "	Oyster "

Wooden, Willow and Stone Ware.

Cedar Buckets,	Stable Brooms,
Painted "	Shaker "
Sugar "	Hearth "
Stable "	Sifters,
Tubs,	Demijohns,
10 gallon Kegs,	Jugs,
5 " "	Jars,
Washboards,	Milk Crocks,
Clothes Baskets,	Churns,
Market "	Butter Firkins,
Work "	

LIQUORS.

Bourbon Whisky,	Concord Wine,
Irish "	Madeira "
Scotch "	Port "
French Brandy, very fine	Sherry "
Apple "	Cooking "
Peach "	Delaware "
Cooking "	Catawba "
London Porter,	Champagne [Cliquot],
Holland Gin,	Sparkling Catawba,
Cidar Vinegar,	Claret,
Blackberry Cordial,	Scotch Ale,
Jamaica Rum,	

☞ We have a very fine article of NATIVE WINE made from the "Concord Grape," which is superior to any Native Wine heretofore offered.

☞ Pure and unadulterated BOURBON WHISKY, of the best quality, bottled for family use.

SUNDRIES.

Cheese,	Corn Starch,
Pine Apple Cheese,	Spices of all kinds,
Sap Sago ",	Table Salt,
Maccaroni (Italian),	Lard (in Caddies),
" (American),	Bristol Brick,
Vermicelli,	Truffles,
Molasses and Syrups,	"Pate de foix Gras,"
Parafine Candles,	Tapioca Farina (new),
Star "	Baking Powders,
Tallow "	Cocoa,
Portable Lemonade,	Chocolate,
Parlor Matches,	Gelatine,
Gunpowder,	Rice,
Shot,	Barley (Pearl),
Sal Soda,	Flavoring Syrups,
Coal Oil,	Concentrated Lye,
Scrubbing Brushes,	" Potash,
Blacking "	Finest Quality of Flour.

—A SMALL LOT OF—

"Fruits and Flowers" Smoking Tobacco.

☞ Our wagon is always ready to deliver goods, bought from us, anywhere in the city limits, free of charge.

WARFIELD & CO.,
Cheapside.

to a very large and attentive audience."[27] After many years use the old meeting house, which faced on Short Street, was razed during the summer and fall of 1913. The present cut-stone church was built on the site, but faces on West Main Street.

The cornerstone of the large and handsome St. Paul's Catholic Church, with its tall tower (210 feet high), now standing on West Short Street facing Spring Street, was laid on November 12, 1865, by the Rt. Rev. G. A. Carroll, bishop of Covington. The church was dedicated Sunday, October 18, 1868; Bishop McGill of Richmond, Va., celebrated the pontificial high mass and Archbishop Purcell of Cincinnati delivered the address.[28] Messrs. Picket & Son, Cincinnati, were the architects; Julian S. Hoagland of Lexington was the builder.

Ashland Agricultural Works, a large brick building "sixty by one hundred and forty-three feet, two stories high, with tower three stories" was completed in the fall of 1868, near the Henry Clay mansion.[29] This was the mechanical shop of the newly-established A. & M. College of Kentucky, which was equipped for the manufacture of various agricultural and farming machinery. The local press said: "This is by far the largest manufacturing establishment about Lexington." Here about 100 young men were given the opportunity to learn a trade and at the same time earn money to help pay for their education. This building served as the mechanical department until the college moved in 1882 to the present University of Kentucky campus. The old building, razed about 1908-10, stood at what is now 133 Sycamore Road, facing east.

1869

On January 29, 1869, the Lexington & Big Sandy Railroad was reorganized and chartered as the Elizabethtown, Lexington & Big Sandy Railroad.[30] By March, 1872, the first rail was laid on Water Street and by the end of the year the road was completed from Lexington to the Big Sandy River, a distance of 109 miles. The line was acquired by the Chesapeake & Ohio Railroad prior to 1880.

At the close of the Civil War there developed a northern and a southern faction in each of the two Presbyterian churches in Lexington. On May 14, 1869, it was agreed that the southern groups should unite to form one church and the northern factions another, the property to be divided according to membership.[31] Accordingly, the southern group acquired the First Presbyterian Church at Broadway and Second Street, valued at $25,000, while the northern faction became owner of the Second Presbyterian Church, figured at $45,000, on the east side of Market Street, between Church and Second streets.

William B. Munson, of Astoria, Illinois, received the first degree, Bachelor of Science, conferred by the Agricultural & Mechanical College of Kentucky, in June, 1869. Next year his brother, T. Volnew Munson, received the second degree.

In the fall of 1869, James M. Hocker, a local banker, established Hocker Female College, "a boarding school of high order for girls." At a cost of about $100,000 Hocker erected a large, four-story brick building on a six-acre campus on the west side of North Broadway, near Fifth Street.[32] Robert Graham was the first president. In 1878, William Hamilton donated $10,000 to the school and it became Hamilton Female College. In its heyday the school had registered 226 students from thirteen states. During the 1920s Transylvania University operated Hamilton as a junior college and used the building in the thirties as a dormitory for girls. When the century-old building was demolished in October, 1962, it was known as Lyons-Hamilton Hall.

The Louisville, Cincinnati & Lexington Railroad came into existence on September 7, 1869, by a merger of the Lexington & Frankfort and the Louisville & Frankfort railroads. Later, on July 1, 1881, the road was purchased by the Louisville & Nashville Railroad and became a part of the eastern division of that road.

Notes

1. The central portion of the University of Kentucky campus.
2. Clark, *A History of Kentucky*, p. 186.
3. *Louisville Public Journal*, October 6, 1852.
4. *Lexington Herald-Leader*, November 16, 1947.
5. Oldham & Hemingway *vs.* Abraham Lincoln, et. al. Fayette Circuit Court, file No. 1268, May 12, 1853.
6. *Kentucky Statesman*, October 13, 1854.
7. *Ibid.*, December 5, 1854.
8. The Britling Apartments were razed during the summer of 1961.
9. *Kentucky Statesman*, February 16, 1855.
10. *Ibid.*, August 17, 1855.
11. *Ibid.*, January 16, 1857.
12. *Lexington Observer & Reporter*, May 16, 1857.
13. *Ibid.*, July 14, 1858.
14. Coleman, *Slavery Times in Kentucky*, p. 166.
15. Ranck, *History of Lexington*, pp. 384-385.
16. This camp was named for Simon B. Buckner, later Brig. General, CSA.
17. *Cincinnati Commercial*, September 4, 1862.
18. *The Vidette*, Springfield, Tenn., Nov. 2, 1862. This small newssheet was published "semi-occasionally" by Morgan's command.
19. *Daily Lexington Transcript*, November 14, 1882.
20. John McMurtry *vs.* Trustees of Transylvania University, Fayette Circuit Court, file No. 966, June 2, 1841.
21. Original funeral invitation in author's collection.
22. The Clay Monument was completed and dedicated July 4, 1861.
23. *Lexington Leader*, September 19, 1952.
24. This building was demolished in June, 1960; Transylvania's Haupt Humanities Building now occupies the site.
25. *Lexington Herald*, December 5, 1945.
26. *Kentucky Gazette*, January 22, 1868.
27. *Ibid.*, July 8, 1868.
28. *Ibid.*, October 21, 1868.
29. *Ibid.*, October 24, 1868.
30. *Acts*, Kentucky Legislature, 1869.
31. *Lexington Observer & Reporter*, May 15, 1869.
32. *Kentucky Gazette*, September 18, 1869.

1870-1889

After the War — Progress

Two contrasting institutions — churches and banks — were indicators of the growth boom that began again following the end of the War Between the States. Passenger train service to distant cities, telephone exchanges, streetcars, electric lights, and a water company were introduced to the people of Lexington.

1870

The Grand Lodge Hall, Independent Order of Odd Fellows, on the north side of West Main (115-19) between Upper and Limestone streets, was dedicated on February 3, 1870 by Grand Master S. S. Fry. This three-story building was built of Ohio freestone with a Mansard roof. The lodge room on the third floor is 58 feet deep, 38½ feet wide and has a high Gothic arched ceiling. Hoagland and Farley were the contractors; Cincinnatus Shryock was the architect. The building is still standing.

Headley & Anderson's Bank was organized March 15, 1870, on Short Street.

On May 6, 1870, the trustees of the First Presbyterian Church sold their building (built in 1857) at the southwest corner of Broadway and Second Street for $15,000 to an offshoot of the Main Street Christian Church, which became Broadway Christian Church. Two years later the Presbyterians moved to a new building at 174 North Mill Street.

On June 7, 1870, the Historical Society of Fayette County was organized in the Lexington Library, with George Robertson, president and Dr. Robert Peter, secretary. Its object was "to preserve and collect the history of Fayette County and the State and to publish manuscripts concerning the county."

On the north corner of Church Street and Broadway stands the handsome brick Centenary Methodist Church, designed by Cincinnatus Shryock. It was built during 1869-70, and formally dedicated on Sunday, July 24, 1870. This church was erected by a group which had split off from the Hill Street Methodist Church and adhered to the northern Conference. In 1955, Centenary united with the Trinity Methodist Church and moved to a new building at 1716 South Limestone Street.

Fayette National Bank was organized September 8, 1870, in a building on the corner of Short and Upper Streets, with Squire Bassett, president.

The *Lexington Press* was founded in October, 1870, by Col. Hart Foster and Maj. Henry T. Duncan as Lexington's first daily newspaper. In January, 1895, it was consolidated with the *Lexington Transcript* which had begun in 1876. The combined paper was known as the *Lexington Daily Press-Transcript,* until the name was changed to the *Morning Herald.* The editorship was placed in the hands of Desha Breckinridge in 1897, where it remained until 1935. The paper's name was changed in 1905 to the *Lexington Herald* and has always been a Democratic organ politically.

During the fall of 1870, Madison C. Johnson, J. W. Kearney and "a number of people in Lexington," ordered "200 pairs of English sparrows," which were claimed "to exterminate caterpillars, worms & mosquitoes."[1] Next year the paper complained that the birds were multiplying too fast and becoming a general nuisance.

The Drake Hotel, a large and popular three-story brick hotel on the north side of Short Street, between Broadway and Mill, was erected around 1870. Two years later a new front was added. It was also known as the Ashland House and Reed Hotel. J. W. Alexander was the early proprietor of this hostelry which, in 1873, was listed as being at "15 West Short Street, opposite the Post Office." In 1878, the spire of the hotel was struck by lightning. The old hostelry was demolished in 1960 to make way for a parking lot.

G. D. Wilgus, Lexington brick manufacturer and contractor, erected the four-story St. Nicholas Hotel in 1870 on the south side of East Main Street several doors west of Limestone.[2] Henry Wolf was the first proprietor. This popular hostelry was later called the Florentine, Leonard and Henry Clay hotels. The building was razed in July, 1947.

The National Exchange Bank, incorporated in 1870, was first located on the north side of Main Street, between Mill and Broadway. It afterward moved to the southeast corner of Main and Mill streets where it remained until its assets were merged with the Central Bank (not the present Central Bank & Trust Company).

DeLong & Brother offered for sale the "New Style Corn Planter for 1870" in this advertisement. DeLong's Main Street office is shown in the picture on page 52.

This year the city's population was placed at 14,801.

1871

Lt. Hugh McKee, native of Lexington and an 1866 Annapolis graduate, was one of three Americans killed in a three-day war between the United States and Cho-Sen, "the hermit kingdom," now called Korea.[3] The inscription on his monument in the Lexington Cemetery reads: "Killed in the attack upon the forts of Corea [sic], made by the U.S. Naval forces June 11, 1871." Lexington's post of the Veterans of Foreign Wars was named for Lt. McKee.

Phantom Lodge No. 15 Knights of Pythias, was organized in Lexington on October 25, 1871, with J. T. Uppington, W.C., and Thomas T. Forman, R.S. This lodge, with Phoenix Lodge No. 25, met for a number of years in the Odd Fellows Grand Lodge Hall at 115-119 West Main near Limestone.

In 1871, 52 acres of the Kentucky Agricultural & Mechanical Association, whose buildings had burned during the Civil War, were sold to the City of Lexington. This became a city park, and in 1882 was given to the Agricultural & Mechanical College of Kentucky which moved there and later became the University of Kentucky.

1872

The First Presbyterian Church, having sold its meeting house at the corner of Broadway and Second, purchased a tract of land on the east side of North Mill Street between Church and Second, and erected a new edifice, designed by Cincinnatus Shryock. It was formally dedicated on May 5, 1872. Total cost of the lot, building, and fixtures was approximately $50,000. The present building is 58 feet wide and 85 feet long including the buttresses; the height of the spire is 180 feet. The oldest congregation in Lexington worships in this church at 174 North Mill Street.

Sons of Temperance, Lexington Division No. 35, was organized on July 29, 1872, in Kastle's Building on West Main Street between Mill and Broadway.

A U.S. Weather Bureau office was established in Lexington in October, 1872, and was in continuous service from 1887 to its closing on July 31, 1933. Various offices housed the bureau; the tower on top of the Administration Building at the University of Kentucky, the Carty Building at Main and Mill, and the Fayette (now First Security) Bank Building. George B. Wurtz was meterologist for many years. The office was re-established at Blue Grass Field in 1944.

On the morning of December 12, "The handsome country residence of David S. Coleman, on the Newtown Pike, three miles from town, was burned with all its contents."[4] This Italianate villa, known as Highland Home, and designed by Major Thomas Lewinski, was erected in 1854. It was similar to Glengarry and was the home of the author's grandfather.

Maxwell Place, on the west side of Rose Street between Rose Lane and Clifton Avenue, is the oldest building on the University of Kentucky campus. Erected by Dennis Mulligan in 1872 in the Italianate villa style, the property was acquired in 1917 by the University as a home for its presidents. The century-old residence has been occupied by Drs. Frank L. McVey, Herman L. Donovan, Frank G. Dickey, John W. Oswald, and currently by Dr. Otis A. Singletary. Judge James H. Mulligan, son of the builder and U.S. consul to Samoa, also lived here; he was the author of the well-known poem, *In Kentucky.* Maxwell Place was named for John Maxwell, Lexington pioneer, whose land grant included the present University campus.

Professor George W. Ranck published his *History of Lexington* in a 428-page volume, printed in Cincinnati. Although a valuable work, he includes the highly fictitious story that Lexington was built upon the ruins of an ancient city, hewn out of solid rock, in which mummies of a long-forgotten race were found. There is no

PRESS PRINTING COMPANY,
OF LEXINGTON, KENTUCKY.
No. of Certificate, 16. No. of Shares, 52
This Certifies, That F. Waters
entitled to Five Shares of the Capital Stock of the
PRESS PRINTING COMPANY,
Transferable in person or by attorney on the Books of said Company upon the surrender of this Certificate.
Witness the signatures of the President and Cashier.
Lexington, Ky., Apr. 26 1873
H. T. Duncan Jr. President.
H Haney. Cashier.

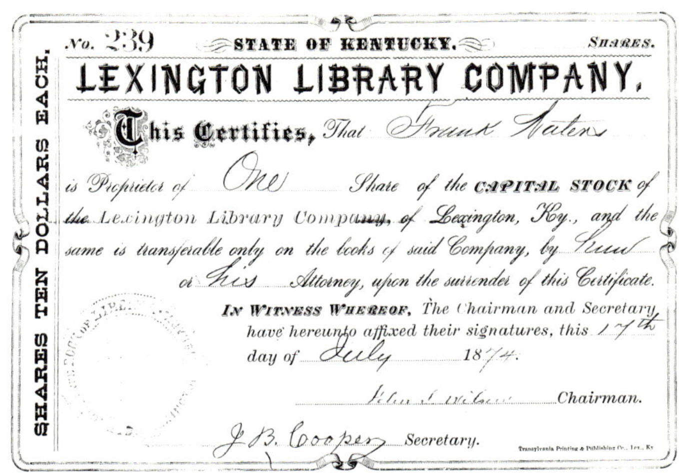
SHARES TEN DOLLARS EACH.
No. 239 STATE OF KENTUCKY. SHARES.
LEXINGTON LIBRARY COMPANY.
This Certifies, That Frank Waters
is Proprietor of One Share of the CAPITAL STOCK of the Lexington Library Company, of Lexington, Ky., and the same is transferable only on the books of said Company, by him or his Attorney, upon the surrender of this Certificate.
IN WITNESS WHEREOF, The Chairman and Secretary have hereunto affixed their signatures, this 17th day of July 1874.
Chairman.
J. B. Cooper Secretary.
Transylvania Printing & Publishing Co., Lex., Ky.

Two stock certificates reflect Lexingtonians' interest in investing in the city's growth.

truth to Ranck's story or his statement that Lexington "was built upon the dust of a dead metropolis of a lost race."

In 1872, through a merger of the Kentucky Agricultural & Mechanical Association with the Maxwell Spring Company, a more effectual organization was formed, known as the Kentucky Agricultural & Mechanical Society. Its first fair was held in September in the woodland of Henry Clay's Ashland, near the city limits. General William Preston was elected president of the new society.

1873

Lexington's seventh city directory, titled: *Sheppard's Lexington City Directory for 1873-74,* was published this year by J. S. Sheppard & Company, Heineman & Lipphardt, printers, Cincinnati. This directory is hardbound and contains 254 pages.

1874

Edward Troye, the noted animal and portrait painter, was born July 12, 1808, in Lausanne, Switzerland. He came to America as a young man, painted pictures of thoroughbred horses all over the South, and after marrying Miss Cornelia Ann Van de Graff, of Scott County, settled in Woodford County. Troye frequently exhibited his horse and "cattle pieces" in Lexington. Late in life, he lived with Keen Richards, near Georgetown, dying there on July 25, 1874. He is buried in the Georgetown Cemetery, with his wife and grandson, Clarence D. Johnson.

Maxwell Place at the University of Kentucky (described at left).

Nottnagle's Flour Mill, still standing at the southeast corner of Walnut and Clark streets, was erected in 1874 by the Nottnagle Brothers to replace an earlier frame one that burned. In this two-story brick mill were made "white or patent flour, Graham Bread, mill feed of various kinds and corn meal." The milling business ceased about 1901.

In the years 1874 through 1889, the Lexington Post Office was located in the two-story brick building (later Vogt & Foley grocery) at the northwest corner of Broadway and Short streets, former site of the Broadway Hotel. Gen. Samuel Woodson Price, soldier and portrait painter, served as postmaster from 1869 to 1876, and Col. Hubbard K. Milward, from 1876 to January 1888. The building was torn down in 1941.

Out West Main Street, opposite the Lexington Cemetery, is Calvary Catholic Cemetery, established in 1874. When the cemetery opened, choice lots sold from $60 to $125.[5] It contains 57 acres of ground of which sixty per cent is developed. As of March 1, 1972, there had been approximately 8,500 interments in this cemetery. The brick gatehouse was built in 1887, and the iron fence and gate put up in 1921.

1875

On January 14, 1875, a second Baptist church was formed in the city, and the next month took the name Pilgrim Baptist Church. The congregation on October 14, 1877, dedicated a large, three-story brick building at the southwest corner of Upper and Church streets. The church was then named the Upper Street Baptist Church and services were held here until March, 1903.[6] Next year the congregation moved to the southwest corner of East High Street and Rodes Avenue and became the Calvary Baptist Church; it then erected (1905) a large stone church on this site which is still standing.

In the spring of 1871, fourteen "dissenters" from the Main Street

A new fire steamer was the occasion for this rare photograph in a view from 1875. Names on the print from Transylvania's Old Library are from left: Joe Bealert (whiskers), George Searcy, Bud Searcy, Andy McNarnee (sitting), Pat Rogers (in derby), James Gilroy, A. J. Tweedy, William Metcalf, James Boylen (driving), Chief Paul Conlon, Sam, Steve Sharp, and Squire Royalty.

Christian Church organized the Second Christian Church and in May, 1874,[7] began the erection of a large church with tower, still standing on the south side of Constitution Street (now East Second Street). The church, which cost $14,000, was dedicated on May 1, 1875. After a few years the congregation became burdened with debt and difficulties arose; on August 10, 1880, the church was sold for $5,000 to a Negro congregation which still uses the building. Today it is known as the East Second Street Christian Church.

On May 25, 1875, Lexington suffered a big fire which originated in the livery stable of Davis and Adams near the corner of Short and Limestone. All the buildings and stores on the east side of Limestone from Short to Main, and several structures on Short Street were lost, including the livery stable and 15 horses.

This year appeared Lexington's eighth city directory, by James H. Prather, titled: *Prather's Lexington City Directory for 1875 and 1876,* in a hardbound book of 299 pages. This was printed by the Transylvania Printing and Publishing Co., Lexington.

This year Stephen G. Gross established a "Pleasure Resort & Beer Garden" on the north side of East Sixth Street, 200 yards east of North Limestone. During the summer months Gross' Park was a favorite resort for the city people, with band concerts and other forms of amusements. The garden was in operation for a number of years.

1876

After its buildings burned and the land was sold to the city for a park, the Kentucky Agricultural & Mechanical Association purchased a 62-acre tract off South Broadway, laid out a race course and built an elaborate grandstand. On August 31, 1876, its first annual fair was held here, lasting five days.[8] This property came to be known as the Fair Grounds, where trotting races, horse shows, circuses, carnivals and other events are held. In 1882, the octagonal Floral Hall, designed by John McMurtry, and still standing, was erected.

During the year 1876, Wilbur R. Smith and his brother started the Commercial College of Kentucky (Transylvania) University in the Melodeon Hall at the southwest corner of Upper and Main streets. Later, the school occupied quarters in the Carty Building at Main and Mill streets. Courses were offered in bookkeeping, handwriting and telegraphy, and the school's enrollment during its heyday numbered several hundred students.

The Farmers & Traders Bank was chartered this year.

Judge George Robertson's autobiography, titled: *An Outline of the Life of George Robertson,* was printed by the Transylvania Printing & Publishing Company. Robertson, familiarly known as "Old Buster," was one of Lexington's noted lawyers and a professor at Transylvania Law College.

1877

Joel T. Hart, Kentucky's foremost sculptor, was born February 11, 1810, in Clark County. As a young man he came to Lexington and worked in Prudens's "marble factory." Without formal training, Hart made the transition from stonecutting to modeling with remarkable ease. He made busts of a number of prominent Kentuckians including Cassius M. Clay, John J. Crittenden, three full-length statues of Henry Clay and his masterpiece, "Woman Triumphant," upon which he labored for 15 years. Hart died in Florence, Italy, on March 2, 1877; his remains were later removed to the Frankfort Cemetery.

On July 23, 1877, the first passenger train ran over the entire length of the Cincinnati Southern Railroad from Cincinnati to Lexington to Somerset, a distance of 157.5 miles. The railroad was built and owned by the City of Cincinnati, and skirted Lexington on its southern city limits. To cross the Kentucky River, the railroad built High Bridge, said to have been the first "cantilever" bridge in the United States. It is 1,125 feet long and the rail elevation is 317 feet above water level. The bridge was built during the years 1876-1877. Lexington passenger service over the Southern Railroad was discontinued several years ago.

Lexington's ninth city directory was published this year in Lexington by R. C. Hellrigle & Company, with the title: *Lexington City Directory and Gazetteer, Cincinnati Southern Railway,* 1877-78, in a hardbound book of 165 pages. The Lexington Public Library owns a copy of this rare directory. From this date on the city directories were published every two or three years.

In 1877, Sister Euphrasia of the Sisters of Charity of Nazareth founded the St. Joseph Hospital in the former Goodloe house, Elley Villa, at 320 Linden Walk near Maxwell Street. In October, 1878, the hospital moved to a large residence on the south side of West Second Street near Georgetown Street. Several additions were made in 1885. Another three-story brick wing was built in 1887, with the annex put on in 1898. The central part, a four-story red brick building with columns, was erected in 1906-08.

Floral Hall (described at left) stands on the Fair Grounds tract off South Broadway now popularly known as the "Red Mile."

Joel T. Hart's "Woman Triumphant," pictured in its case in the courthouse, was destroyed when the building burned in 1897.

1878

On March 13, 1878, by an act of the Kentucky legislature, the Agricultural & Mechanical College of Kentucky was severed from Kentucky (Transylvania) University. Thus a new college was created, free from all sectarian or denominational control, to stand on its own legs. The City of Lexington gave its city park (52 acres) on South Limestone Street as a home for the A. & M. College, together with $30,000 in bonds for building purposes to which Fayette County added $20,000. The state school rented for two years its former quarters and grounds at Ashland and the Woodlands until suitable buildings could be erected on its new campus.

1879

On April 2, 1879, Lexington celebrated the one hundredth anniversary of the settlement of the town "with great demonstrations of rejoicing." The day was ushered in by a 100-gun salute from brass six-pounders belonging to the volunteer artillery company. There was a mile long parade with citizens dressed as Indians, pioneers, Continental soldiers, and figures from the city's history. Main Street never contained so many people at one time, and "there was a press and jam everywhere."[9] The parade disbanded on the Transylvania University campus where the exercises were continued in Morrison Chapel; addresses were given by Gov. James B. McCreary, General Leslie Combs, Judge Ben P. Buckner and others. 9 The celebration was described by an eastern newspaper as "the grandest thing of the kind ever seen in Central Kentucky."

On Wednesday, May 14, 1879, the fourth day of the spring races, when the city was full of out-of-town sportsmen, the Phoenix Hotel was destroyed by fire; the loss was estimated at $150,000. Also destroyed in the blaze were Treacy & Wilson's livery stable and the residence of General Leslie Combs. At the time of the fire, the old hostelry, originally Postlethwait's Tavern, was a commodious three-story brick building on the site of the present Phoenix Hotel. Famous guests who had lodged here included Presidents Andrew Jackson, James Monroe, William H. Harrison and Chester A. Arthur, the Marquis de Lafayette, Amos Kendall, Generals Braxton Bragg, E. Kirby Smith, U. S. Grant and Santa Anna of Mexico.

Jackson Hall, a large two-story red brick building and Lexington's sixth market house, was erected in 1879 at a cost of $18,000. This structure was on the site of two earlier market houses and covered the entire block from Limestone to Upper and from Vine to Water streets. The upper floor of Jackson Hall was given over to the offices of city government; the lower floor had stalls inside facing a central passageway which ran the length of the building. In later years, the second floor was used for shows, exhibitions and other forms of amusements. Over the main entrance on Limestone an iron plaque read: "Jackson Hall, 1879." P. L. Lundin was the architect for this market house. In 1941, David Ades bought

Jackson Hall (described above).

the property for $40,000 and shortly thereafter razed the building for a parking lot.

1880

The first football game west of the Alleghenies was played on April 9, 1880, between Kentucky (Transylvania) University and Centre College of Danville. The contest was staged on a field of the city park about where McLean Stadium stands on Euclid Avenue. The game was a combination of soccer and rugby football and five hundred people witnessed it. After two hours play the final score was Kentucky University 13-¾ to Centre's O.[10] Next year the teams played in Danville with the result: Center 5¼ to Kentucky University's ½. Each team used 15 players in its lineup.

At 11 o'clock, July 1, 1880, "professor" W. N. Lake began his "walkathon," and every half hour thereafter walked a half mile, about four times around the courthouse square. He kept this up for sixteen days and six hours. At 5 P.M., on July 17, Lake terminated his pedestrial feat, having walked "780 half miles in 780 consecutive half hours."[11] Fully three thousand people gathered on Cheapside to see him terminate "his wonderful feat of strength and powers of endurance." To show that he was still going strong, Lake, as he neared the end of his walk, picked up six-year-old William Beasley and a forty-pound gun, and carried them on his shoulders for several rounds.

Professor W. N. Lake.

As the center of Kentucky's largest hemp-growing section, Lexington had a number of hemp factories from 1880 through 1910. Some of the larger ones were H. B. Nelson & Bro., 309 East Main; Richard C. Morgan & Company, 276 West Main; Brucetown Hemp Factory, northwest corner Limestone and Loudoun; James F. Scott & Brother, 149 West Third; Avery S. Winston, 128-34 North Broadway; Lexington Cordage Company, 272 West Short; J. Percy Scott & Son, 60 West Third; R. R. Sparks Hemp Factory, 276-78 West Main; and John W. Frazer & Company, east side of North Broadway, south of Third Street. These companies manufactured cotton bagging, burlap sacks, rope, twine, oakum and other products from the hemp fibers.

Asbury M. E. Church, a one-story red brick church with quoins on the front sides, stood at the northeast corner of Mill and High streets. It was erected in 1880-82; John McMurtry was the architect. The building was razed in November, 1969. This church was the outgrowth of the African Methodist Church, built in 1850 on Vine Street.

This year the city's population was figured to be 16,487 persons.

1881

On October 3, 1881, King Kalakaua of the Sandwich Islands arrived in Lexington for a three-day visit. He was the only foreign sovereign to have visited here.[12]

The first train over the Chesapeake & Ohio Railroad from Ashland to Lexington arrived on December 12, 1881, using part of the old Lexington & Big Sandy tracks which had been in the process of construction off and on since 1852. Sometime previous to 1880, the latter road was extended from Lexington to Louisville. In 1882, the C. & O Railroad erected a two-story red brick passenger station on South Limestone and Water streets, in back of the Phoenix Hotel. This was used until 1907 when Union Station on East Main Street was completed.

Dudley School No. 3, still standing at the northeast corner of Mill and Maxwell streets, was completed in 1881 and named for Dr. Benjamin W. Dudley, a local surgeon. The building has not been used for school purposes since the early 1930s.

1882

The Agricultural & Mechanical College of Kentucky moved from Ashland and the Woodlands to its new 52 acre campus on South Limestone Street on February 13, 1882, when three buildings were completed. These were the three-story brick Administration Building, the two-story brick residence for President James K. Patterson, and the four-story brick dormitory (White Hall) for boys. The state institution was often called Kentucky State College, or simply State College, and later State University. Only the Administration Building remains today.

In the spring of 1882, the first telephone service was inaugurated in Lexington, with the exchange located on the third floor of a building on Cheapside near Short Street. Ben Freckman and Henry Miller were the day and night telephone operators.

The Board of Commerce was established this year with Avery S. Winston, banker and hemp manufacturer, the first president.

On July 17, 1882, the Western Electric Light Company was chartered and used as its first plant, a small room on Vine Street behind the C. S. Brent Seed Company on South Broadway at Vine Street. Shortly afterwards a few arc lights were strung up along Main Street replacing the earlier artificial gas lights.

On August 12, 1882, the first mule-drawn street cars made their appearance on the streets of Lexington. Nine miles of track were laid, 30 mules and 15 small wooden cars were purchased; this constituted the total equipment of the early transportation system. Runs were made to several points in the city. An extra mule was hitched in tandem to the street cars ascending the South Broadway hill. On September 11, 1883, fire destroyed the car barns and mule sheds at Fourth and Race streets with the loss of 59 mules, two horses and 14 cars.[13] In the spring of 1890, the mule-drawn car system went out of business, after having served the city for seven and one-half years.

Mule-drawn street cars at Woodland Park.

Architect Thomas Lewinski (with beard) in a photograph made by Lexington's noted photographer Isaac Jenks.

Major Thomas Lewinski, soldier of fortune, Polish emigré, and ante-bellum architect, died at his home on East Main Street September 18, 1882. He was the designer of a number of fine homes, including Glengarry, the reconstructed Ashland, the front addition to Cassius M. Clay's White Hall in Madison County, Christ Episcopal Church, McChord (Second) Presbyterian Church, Clay Villa (James B. Clay house) on Forest Avenue, Mansfield (Thomas M. Clay house) on Richmond Road, the David S. Coleman house (Highland Home) on Newtown Pike, and the gardener's cottage at Ashland. Lewinski was resident engineer for the construction of the Henry Clay monument in the Lexington Cemetery; he also served as drillmaster for John Hunt Morgan's Lexington Rifles. The Polish architect was buried in the Lexington Cemetery where no monument marks his grave.

About this time the Palace Hotel was erected on South Limestone Street and Vine south of the C. & O. and Kentucky Central Railroad depot. It was a three-story brick building, later called the Ritz Hotel, and was for many years the office of the Railway Express Company. This building was razed in the summer of 1969 as part of the Urban Renewal plan. Another hotel, the Savoy, at the northeast corner of Limestone and Short streets was built in the mid-1880s and still stands, although no longer used as a hostelry.

The Woodland Park Association in 1882 purchased 110 acres of the Woodlands, the former home of James Erwin, son-in-law of Henry Clay.[14] About 480 lots were cut off for sale and 15 acres devoted to Woodland Park, where a large frame auditorium with twin towers was erected. Lake Chenosa provided swimming and boating. This was "the principal resort of Lexington." Mule-drawn street cars conveyed visitors to the park entrance on Central Avenue at Park Avenue. Musical concerts, plays, shows, entertainments and the popular Chautauquas were held here each summer. The frame auditorium was demolished in the spring of 1905 and the lake drained in 1906. The last Chautauqua held at the park was on June 24, 1908.

After 1882, the Kentucky Central Railroad abandoned its earlier station near the Lexington Cemetery and used the passenger depot on South Limestone jointly with the C. & O. Railroad. The Louisville, Cincinnati & Lexington (later L. & N.) Railroad used the old three-story brick station of the Lexington & Ohio at the corner of Mill and Vine streets. The Cincinnati Southern had its passenger depot at 701 South Broadway, its present location.

Lell's European Hotel, as it was styled, stands on the west side of North Broadway, one door south of Short Street. This large three-story brick building was erected around 1882, by J. W. Lell, a prominent businessman and caterer. In October, 1904, the property, then known as the Fayette Hotel, was sold for $23,700.[15] In recent years, several hotels have operated here, while the ground floor is devoted to business purposes.

James Lane Allen, Kentucky's man of letters, taught "a select preparatory school for boys" during the years 1882 to 1884 in the Masonic Grand Lodge Hall, at Walnut and Short streets. His private school was limited to 20 young men, and tuition was $40 for a term of five months. After two years as a pedagogue, Mr. Allen devoted his time to novel and short-story writing.

History of Fayette County, Kentucky by William H. Perrin was published by O. L. Baskin, 905 pages, Chicago, Ill. Pages 221-480 contain a history of Lexington by George W. Ranck and Dr. Robert Peter.

Still standing at 410-412 West Short Street, two doors west of Broadway, is Lell's Hall built in 1882. "A variety show and similar performances were conducted every evening" on the second floor, while a beer parlor and restaurant occupied the ground floor. The shows during the mid-1880s were mostly patronized by men. During the early years of this century, the building gained fame as the starting point for Ed "Strangler" Lewis' climb to the world's wrestling championship. Lewis used the second floor as his training quarters when the old theater was converted into a gymnasium.

1883

On February 17, 1883, F. Bush & Son, local contractors, bought the old brick courthouse (built in 1806) for $1,200, and two days later began tearing it down.[16] To many of the older citizens the razing of this landmark was a sad sight. It had been Lexington's Civil War courthouse. Within its walls echoed the voices of many of Lexington's ablest lawyers and statesmen, including Henry Clay, William T. Barry, Richard H. Menefee, Madison C. Johnson, Thomas F. Marshall, Cassius M. Clay, Joseph Hamilton Daveiss, John C. Breckinridge, James B. Beck and W. C. P. Breckinridge. By March 2, 1883, the site was cleared for the new courthouse, Lexington's fourth.

Lexingtonians at the sheriff's office in 1883 are from left: William Bush, Gip Sammons, E. B. Dishman, Jesse Hall, Col. John R. Graves, Estes Garrett, J. Waller Rhodes, and Judge James R. Jewell. The office was at the east side of the courthouse then under construction.

For the first time residents of the city had free mail delivery, beginning April 1, 1883, from the two-story brick Post Office at the northwest corner of Broadway and Short streets. There were then only five city carriers. The Post Office building later housed Vogt & Foley's grocery. Rural delivery to county boxes (R.F.D.) did not begin until 1889. Fayette County had ten or twelve post offices during the last quarter of the nineteenth century with only one in Lexington.

The Second National Bank opened on County Court Day, April 9, 1883, with David H. James, president; Robert A. Thornton and Jacob H. Graves, vice-presidents; W. D. Nichols, cashier, and J. P. Shaw, teller. The Second National, now Lexington's second oldest bank, has occupied five different buildings, but in 89 years has never been more than 75 yards from its original location at the corner of Cheapside and Short Street. Around 1955 the bank's name was changed to the Second National Bank & Trust Company; Jacob H. Graves is the current president of the bank.

General Ulysses S. Grant stopped off in Lexington June 4, 1883, on his way from Louisville to Washington. He spent a day here, stayed at the Phoenix Hotel, and was driven out to see some of the fine stock farms.[17]

On July 31, 1883, President Chester A. Arthur, with Secretary of State Robert T. Lincoln, Secretary of the Treasury Charles J. Folger, Postmaster General Walter Q. Gresham and other officials, on their way to the Cotton Exposition in Louisville, stopped off in Lexington.[18] The party was entertained by Major H. C. McDowell at Ashland where they saw his fine horses and then went across the road to see those of Captain Barney Treacy. After an elaborate reception at the Phoenix Hotel, the presidential party departed by train for Louisville.

The following newspapers were published in Lexington this year: *Lexington Press, Lexington Transcript, Evening News, Kentucky Stock Farm, Kentucky Gazette, Live Stock Record, Lexington Observer, Apostolic Times, Kentucky Republican* and the *Hamilton College Monthly.* Kentucky's first newspaper, *The Kentucky Gazette,* which was revived after the Civil War, was published weekly and semiweekly by Howard Gratz on Cheapside.

In 1883, Lexington had eight banks: David A. Sayre Bank, northeast corner, Short and Mill; Northern Bank, northwest corner, Market and Short; First National Bank, Short Street between Market and Upper; Second National Bank, corner Cheapside and Short; Third National (formerly Grinstead & Bradley Bank), northwest corner of Short and Upper; Lexington City National Bank, northwest corner, Main and Cheapside; Fayette National Bank, northeast corner, Main and Upper, and National Exchange Bank, on Main Street near Mill. The Farmers and Traders Bank, at 32 East Short, had recently gone out of business.

1884

On July 4, 1883, the cornerstone of Lexington's fourth (third on the same site) courthouse was laid and the building was completed in the fall of 1884. The structure cost $112,277, with Thomas W. Boyd, of Pittsburgh, the architect and F. Bush & Son, Lexington, contractors. The plan of the building called for a "cut-stone structure, two stories high, with basement and dome, the floor space being 90 by 117 feet, and 100 feet from the tip of the dome to the ground level." The superstructure was made of wood covered with tin to resemble stone construction.

Main Street and the courthouse around 1885.

During the year 1884, Moses Kaufman, Judge Jere R. Morton, and several others established the Overland Telephone Company, with offices and exchange on Cheapside near Short Street. In December, 1895, the International Telephone Construction Company, and next year the American Telephone & Telegraph Company of Kentucky, held franchises in the city. Finally, on July 9, 1898, the East Tennessee Company bought up the franchises and controlled the telephones in the city until 1901, when the Fayette Home Telephone Company was organized "to fight the trust."

During this year the Lexington Roller Mills built a three-story building on the west side of South Broadway, at Water and Vine streets. Later, an additional two stories were added. The mills were demolished in 1968 as part of the Urban Renewal program.

1885

Gilbert H. King, General William Preston and Colonel R. H. S. Thompson organized the Lexington Hydraulic & Manufacturing Company to provide water for the city. Capital stock was set at $200,000. In July, 1884, convicts were hired by the Mason Company and set to work digging Lake Ellerslie, opposite the Levi Todd home on the Richmond Pike. At 2:30 P.M., on January 30, 1885, the assembled crowds saw firemen throw a two-inch stream of water as high as the weather vane on the new courthouse. This meant the beginning of a new era in Lexington.

1886

Early on the morning of January 15, 1886, the large Odd Fellows Hall, known as the Opera House, at the southeast corner of Main and Broadway, was discovered to be on fire and by noon the building was a complete loss.[19] "Skipped by the Light of the Moon" was the last show given in the opera house on the evening before it burned.

After the Odd Fellows Hall burned on January 15, another three-story brick building was erected on the site. In circular letters near the top, facing Main Street, were the words: "Merrick Lodge No. 31, I. O. O. F." Shortly after its completion, the building was taken over and used for years by the C. F. Brower Company, dealers in fine furniture, carpets, wall paper and draperies. In later years, it has been occupied by the Sleepy Head House, and is now its headquarters.

The Security Trust & Safety Vault Company was incorporated April 9, 1886, by Madison C. Johnson and a number of prominent

The "programme" from an Opera House production.

OPERA HOUSE.

Thursday Night, Sept. 12th.

GRAND CONCERT

FOR THE BENEFIT OF THE

Yellow Fever Sufferers!

Given by the BEST AMATEUR TALENT of this and adjoining cities, under the

Management of Mr. R. de Roode.

PROGRAMME.

PART FIRST.

1. Piano Duet—Radieuse . . . . Gottschalk
2. Vocal Quartette—Sunrise . . . . White
3. Aria—O Mio Fernando, from La Favorita . . . . . Donizetti
4. Piano Solo—Trembling Leaves . . . . Wehli
5. Vocal Solo—Ave Maria . . . . Dudley Buck
6. Nautical Ballad—Nancy Lee . . . . English
7. Piano Solo—Rondo Capriccioso . . . . Mendelssohn
8. Ballad—Farewell . . . . Graham

PART SECOND.

9. Vocal Duett—Si la Stanchezza, from Il Trovatore . . . Verdi
10. Piano Solo—Grand Waltz, op. 34, No. 1 . . . . . . Chopin
11. Ballad—The two Grenadiers . . . . Schumann
12. Ballad—The Harp that once thro' Tara's Hall . . . . ———
13. Piano Solo—Saltarelle . . . . Haberbier
14. Ballad—The Village Blacksmith's Bride . . . . ———
15. Vocal Trio—Te Sol, from Attila . . . . Verdi

☞The magnificent Concert Grand Piano which will be used, is from the celebrated manufactory of Hazelton Brothers, New York.

General Admission, - - - 50 Cents.
Reserved Seats, - - - 75 Cents.

TO BE HAD AT BARNES & WOOD'S DRUG STORE.

Secure your tickets early for a Concert the like of which you will not hear again.
R. de ROODE.

business men. Capital stock was set at $100,000. Ephraim D. Sayre was president and W. L. Threlkeld, secretary-treasurer. Around 1893 the bank erected a four-story brick building at No. 7 East Short Street and occupied it for the next 10 or 11 years.

The Kentucky Union Railroad was built to reach the rich coal and timber resources of southeastern Kentucky. Construction was begun in 1886, and 14.7 miles were completed that year. The line extended west from Lexington in 1890 and east to Jackson in 1891, a distance of 92 miles. On March 11, 1894, the line, having been placed in receivership, was purchased for one million dollars by J. Kennedy Tod & Company, who reorganized it as the Lexington & Eastern Railway. In 1910, the L. & N. Railroad purchased the entire stock of the L. & E., which five years later went out of business. Subsequently, in 1911, the line extended to McRoberts, approximately 100 miles beyond Jackson.

The new Opera House was begun in 1886 and completed in 1887 at a cost of $45,000; Herman L. Rowe was the architect. It stands on the west side of North Broadway, between Short and Second streets, opposite the Masonic Temple. On August 19, 1887, the Opera House was formally opened with Lizzie Evan's presentation of "Our Angel." Opera made its debut on October 14, when Emma Abbott gave the comedy "The Mikado." Lexington long had the reputation of being "the best one-night stand in the nation," and many famous actors and actresses have played here, including Maude Adams, Julia Harlow, Otis Skinner, Helen Hayes, George Arliss and Mrs. Leslie Carter. For a number of years the Lexington Opera House has had only motion picture shows.

1887

In the spring of 1887, the birthplace of Mary Todd, future wife of Abraham Lincoln, was purchased by St. Paul's Catholic Church and was torn down by local contractors Albert Howard and George Clark. The bricks and other materials, including the stairway, windows and doors, were used to construct the two-story gatehouse still standing at the entrance to Calvary Cemetery, 874 West Main Street.

The Opera House on North Broadway (described above).

The Calvary Cemetery house (described above).

In 1887, Professor A. N. Gordon started Alleghan Academy, a select day and boarding school for boys in the ante-bellum house (Mrs. C. W. Burt's) on the Nicholasville Pike several hundred yards south of Southland Drive. Beginning in September, 1887, the school operated for thirteen years. The old house was demolished in December, 1966.

On the morning of November 16, 1887, Colonel Thomas M. Green of Maysville shot and killed Colonel Lewis D. Baldwin of Nicholasville in front of the Phoenix Hotel.[20] Both were newspapermen and had been enemies for some time over letters Green had published in the *Commercial Gazette* regarding voting procedures. Five or six shots passed between the two men. Baldwin was carried into the hotel and died in a few minutes; Green received only a flesh wound in the left side.

On November 16, 1887, the full-length statue of John C. Breckinridge was unveiled on Cheapside. The Breckinridge Monument Association sponsored the movement; the Kentucky legislature appropriated $10,000, and $4,000 was raised by private funds. Edward L. Valentine of Richmond, Virginia was the sculptor. Senator J. C. S. Blackburn gave the memorial address and Governor Simon B. Buckner unveiled the monument. The inscription on the granite base reads: "John Cabell Breckinridge, Erected by the Commonwealth of Kentucky. A. D. 1887." Breckinridge was the youngest vice-president of the United States, and was secretary of war and a general of the Confederate States. He is buried in the Lexington Cemetery.

1888

Lexington Lodge No. 281, Independent Order of Odd Fellows, was established on February 8, 1888. After a number of years of operation it went out of existence.

A photograph of Gratz Park and downtown Lexington from this period includes the hedges and iron gates that surrounded the park at that time. Third Street is just beyond the picket fence in the middle of the photograph. The small round shelter is at the present site of the James Lane Allen fountain now in the north end of the park.

Nancy Anderson, known as Old Boss and formerly a slave, was a unique character around town who made her living as a paper and rag picker. On March 6, 1888, while picking up coal in the L. & N. yards, she was run over by a switch engine; both legs were amputated and she died at the age of 75. A local drugstore named a brand of cigars Old Boss for this eccentric character.

On March 21, 1888, Samuel J. Roberts, Judge George Denny and E. D. Warfield founded the Lexington Leader Printing Company to publish the *Lexington Leader,* a Republican daily newspaper. It was one of the pioneers in the field of specialized news and departments for family reading. In 1937, its owner, John G. Stoll, purchased the *Lexington Herald* and published both papers from the same press without disturbing the political policy or integrity of either. Headquarters for both papers are in the building at the northeast corner of Short and Market streets.

The Phoenix National Bank was organized in 1888, and was located on East Main Street at the Phoenix Alley.

1889

Stagecoach travel in Kentucky reached its heyday during the antebellum days and fairly regular schedules were maintained. A network of routes covered the state and such lines as the Old Reliable, Good Intent and Accomodation Line served the traveling public out of Lexington. During the years several sites were used as the stagecoach office, the last being in the western end of the old three-story Post Office building at the southwest corner of Short and Mill. By 1885, there were only two stagecoach lines operating in the Bluegrass, both owned by Thomas H. Irvine. The last of these, the Lexington & Versailles, made its final run out of the city on January 1, 1889.

On January 28, 1889, nearly 200 members of the Cerneau Scottish Rite gathered in Lexington and established a Grand Consistory of Kentucky, with James L. Watson, Grand Master, and John W. Lancaster, Grand Secretary.[21] Four subordinate consistories were established: Louisville No. 27, Covington No. 30, Frankfort No. 35, and Lexington No. 38. The Cerneau Rite was in direct conflict with the Pike Rite of Scottish Freemasonry which had been established in Kentucky in 1852. After several years agitation, the Grand Lodge of Kentucky declared the Cerneau body "illegal, clandestine and un-Masonic," and outlawed it.

During the years 1887-1889, the U. S. Government erected a fine, three-story stone Post Office and Federal Building at the northwest corner of East Main and Walnut streets. It was completed at a cost of $150,000 and occupied on February 4, 1889. The second floor furnished offices for the collector of internal revenue. The building was abandoned December 20, 1936, and the city purchased it for $400. This Post Office, Lexington's sixth, was demolished in 1941.

On February 24, 1889, St. John's Episcopal Church located on the north side of East Main Street,[22] opposite Rose, was opened for divine services. With a seating capacity for four hundred, the church was a red brick of Norman Gothic design. About forty families were enrolled on the parish register. St. John's Church was demolished in May, 1903, and most of the congregation returned to Christ Church.

In June, 1889, the Womans' Guild of Christ Episcopal Church established a hospital in the Farmer Deweese house (White Cottage) on the north side of East Short Street 200 yards east of Deweese Street. It was known as the Protestant Infirmary. On January 25, 1899, the hospital was incorporated and its name changed to the Good Samaritan. A glass-domed operating room and a three-story brick building were added later.

Col. Bennett H. Young built the Louisville Southern Railroad from Lexington to Louisville in an effort to break the monopoly the L. & N. Railroad had on rail traffic from Louisville to the South and to all of Kentucky east of Louisville. On August 24, 1889, the first train over this road from Louisville to Lexington via Shelbyville, Lawrenceburg, Tyrone and Versailles pulled into the Cincinnati Southern's passenger station on South Broadway in Lexington. Construction of Young's High Bridge over the Kentucky River at Tyrone was completed in 1888-89 at a cost of $245,000. This road was later acquired by the Cincinnati Southern. Passenger service over it was discontinued in the late 1930s; freight service is still operated as far as Lawrenceburg.

Betty Shea, a house servant in the John Woolfolk residence, now the Whitehall Funeral Home at the northeast corner of Third and Limestone streets, was murdered by Tom O'Brien on Sunday night, April 1, 1889.[23] O'Brien and Miss Shea had been married in October, 1888, but this fact had been kept secret. O'Brien, who lived in another part of the city, slipped into the house and killed his wife without awakening the Woolfolk family. He was convicted in the Fayette Circuit Court and hanged on February 27, 1890.

William P. Welsh, noted Kentucky portrait painter was born in Lexington on September 20, 1889. He served in the United States

The Lexington-Versailles stagecoach about 1884.

Lexington artist William P. Welsh, F.R.S.A.

Army in both World Wars and established his studio in Lexington after World War II. Welsh was elected a member of the Royal Society of Arts of Great Britain and has painted many noted Kentuckians and others over the country. His studio is currently at 255 North Broadway.

On November 8, 1889, Col. Armstead Swope and Col. William C. Goodloe happened to arrive at the same time to pick up their mail at the Post Office at the corner of Main and Walnut streets. They were bitter enemies as a result of disagreements at the Republican convention the year before. The postal boxes of the two men were next to each other. After some harsh words had passed, Colonel Swope drew a pistol and Colonel Goodloe a four-inch hunting knife. Swope received 13 stab wounds, while Goodloe was shot in the abdomen.[24] Swope died immediately, and Goodloe two days later.

The present Northern Bank building at the northwest corner of Market and Short streets was erected in 1889, to replace an earlier building erected in 1835. During the spring of 1962 the tower was removed, and other repairs were made to the top of the structure; the interior was also remodeled.

Notes

1. *Kentucky Gazette*, September 3, 1870.
2. *Ibid.*, March 12, 1870.
3. *Ibid.*, August 28, 1871.
4. *Ibid.*, December 14, 1872.
5. *The Lexington Dispatch*, April 20, 1875.
6. *Lexington Morning Herald*, March 20, 1903.
7. *Lexington Press*, May 30, 1874.
8. *Live Stock Record*, Lexington, August 28, 1886.
9. *Frank Leslie's Illustrated Newspaper*, April 26, 1879.
10. *Lexington Transcript*, April 10, 1880.
11. *Lexington Daily Press*, July 18, 1880.
12. *Lexington Transcript*, October 3, 1881.
13. *Ibid.*, September 12, 1883.
14. *Lexington Daily Press*, September 20, 1882.
15. *Lexington Morning Transcript*, October 24, 1904.
16. *Daily Lexington Transcript*, February 19, 1883.
17. *Lexington Transcript*, June 5, 1883.
18. *Lexington Daily Press*, August 1, 1883.
19. *Kentucky Statesman*, January 16, 1886.
20. *Lexington Transcript*, November 17, 1887.
21. *The Courier-Journal*, January 29, 1889.
22. *Lexington Morning Herald*, November 28, 1900. Site of the Mammoth Garage at 333 East Main Street.
23. *Ibid.*, April 2, 1889.
24. *Lexington Daily Press*, November 9, 1889.

1890-1909

Lexington Enjoys Leisure — Kentucky Style

The "gay nineties" did not fail to effect Fayette County. This period saw citizens enjoying moving-pictures, the first state fair, Woodland Park, and staged extravaganzas such as a head-on locomotive collision and a 100-mile bicycle race. The Fayette County courthouse and jail, the Southern Railroad station, and Central Christian Church were erected during this era.

1890

John McMurtry, one of Lexington's noted architects, was born September 13, 1812, on his father's farm on the Iron Works and Russell Cave Pikes five and one-half miles north of Lexington. His best-known works include Ingelside, Elley Villa, Botherum, Kentucky School for the Deaf at Danville, St. Peter's Catholic Church, Episcopal Cemetery Chapel, Transylvania's second medical hall, Paris and Lexington Cemetery gatehouses, Asbury Methodist Church, John McCauley house, Lyndhurst, Maxwell Spring Amphitheater, Lexington & Ohio Railway station, The Elms and the Floral Hall at the Fair Grounds. McMurtry died in Lexington March 3, 1890.

The first electric street car ran on the streets of Lexington on September 1, 1890, the trip being made from the car barn on Loudoun Avenue to the Phoenix Hotel. Construction of lines soon followed so that the city was served with 15-18 miles of street car service. By early summer, a large, three-story brick powerhouse had been completed on the south side of Loudoun between North Broadway and North Limestone Street. This furnished the power for the electric street cars. Lexington's last street car (No. 206) made the final run April 2, 1938, from the car barn to the Lafayette Hotel after motor buses replaced the electric street cars.

The Central Bank was organized as a state bank in 1890 and was located on the northwest corner of Short and Upper streets. This bank and the National Exchange Bank (established 1870) were combined in 1906 to form the Lexington Banking & Trust Company.

1891

Maxwell Street Presbyterian was established as a mission church by the First Presbyterian Church. The congregation built a brick structure on the south side of West Maxwell Street at the corner of Jersey Street. The meeting house cost $7,000, and was dedicated on April 17, 1891. By 1916, the membership had outgrown this building which was sold to the Ohava Zion congregation. The Presbyterians then erected a new and larger building (the present one) at the southwest corner of East Maxwell and Lexington Avenue, which was dedicated on July 2, 1916. This continues to be a prosperous church with a total membership of about 1,150.

The Broadway Christian Church building (built in 1857), which had been purchased in 1870 from the First Presbyterian Church, was torn down in 1891, and a more modern structure was erected on the site at Broadway and Second Street. The cornerstone was laid April 23, 1891,[1] and the building dedicated for divine service on September 20, 1891, with the Rev. A. C. Bartholomew as pastor. A view of this church is shown in *The Church Record* (New York, 1897, p. 41). This church was destroyed by fire on February 27, 1916.

On the north side of East (No. 113) Short Street, about 300 feet east of Limestone, stands the present Fayette County jail, erected in 1891. This three-story stone structure replaced the former jail (Megowan's) at the northwest corner of Limestone and Short streets.

1892

Early in 1892, the old Kentucky Agricultural & Mechanical Society was absorbed by the Kentucky Trotting Horse Breeders Association through its stockholders at a meeting in the Commercial Club. During a race meet that year, the 16-year-old grandstand collapsed, injuring a number of people. Another frame stand was erected a year later which burned on October 7, 1931. It was replaced with the present grandstand, built of steel and concrete. The annual spring and fall trotting races are still held at this historic track, known as the "Red Mile."

On June 1, 1892, Lexington celebrated the 100th anniversary of Kentucky's admission into the federal union. The program began on Cheapside, where the ceremonies were interrupted by a downpour of rain. The crowd adjoined to the courthouse where Gov. John Y. Brown and Col. W. C. P. Breckinridge were among the speakers. Several prominent citizens of Philadelphia came to Lexington by train and presented the state of Kentucky with four oil paintings. Later in the day, burgoo was served in the large frame auditorium at Woodland Park.[2]

1893

The celebrated breach-of-promise case brought by 18-year-old Madeline Pollard, a student at Sayre Female Institute, against Col. W. C. P. Breckinridge, son of the Rev. Dr. Robert J. Breckinridge, was tried in the circuit court at Washington, D. C., in March, 1893. Miss Pollard sued for $50,000; she was awarded $15,000 by the jury. Both parties were residents of Lexington.

Maryland Christian Church, a brick church on the north side of

The Fayette County jail (described above).

Citizens in front of the Phoenix Hotel at the corner of Main and Limestone in this picture made in the 1890s.

Maryland (No. 529) Avenue near Jefferson, was dedicated May 21, 1893, as the Maryland Avenue German Evangelical Church, with a membership of 22. In 1905, the church was purchased by the Temple Adath Israel congregation. In 1924, the Forest Hill Christian Church bought the building and moved into it. Some years later the name was changed to the Northern Heights Christian Church, when that group moved into a new sanctuary at 511 Thurman Drive. In January, 1962, a new congregation acquired the building and is worshipping in the structure under the name, Maryland Christian Church, Inc.

A group from the Main Street Christian Church erected the present church with tower on the site of the Grand Masonic Hall, at the northeast corner of Walnut and Short streets. The cornerstone of the Central Christian Church was laid on August 7, 1893,[3] and the new stone church was dedicated July 22, 1894. F. L. and E. E. Smith were the architects; the builder was John H. Walker, and the cost was $60,000. About this time the church changed its name to the Central Christian Church, its present designation.

The Leland Hotel, on the south side of West Short Street (opposite Woolcott's Garage) near Limestone, was opened for business on November 25, 1893, with 46 guest rooms.[4] Later more stories were added. The old hotel was razed about 1965.

In 1893, the *Kentucky Leader* criticized the city for desecrating the "old city cemetery" on the south side of Bolivar Street opposite South Mill Street.[5] John Maxwell gave the ground for a burial site and it became known as Maxwell's Graveyard. Some early settlers were buried here, including John Maxwell and his wife Sarah;

Rev. Robert Cloud; Mrs. Elizabeth Ridgley, wife of Dr. Frederick Ridgley; William Satterwhite; Jane Mekins; Anna McLean and others. This old cemetery was later sold to the Van Orsdel Spoke Company and the Lexington Wheel Company, both of which erected factories on the site. Many of the old tombstones were broken up and used in the foundations of the buildings. Currently the burial site is occupied by a tobacco redrying factory.

1894

The House of Mercy, a charitable institution now known as the Florence Crittenton Home for unwed mothers, was opened February 6, 1894, at 519 West Fourth Street, near Jefferson. It is still in operation in a large, two-story brick residence.

The Lexington & Eastern Railroad, from Lexington to Jackson, a distance of 92 miles, was the outgrowth of the Kentucky Union Railroad which had been sold at auction in March, 1894. It was reorganized as the Lexington & Eastern. In 1910, the L. & N. Railroad purchased the entire stock of the L. & E., and five years later, in 1915, the line went out of business.

On Saturday, May 19, 1894, Lexington and Fayette County experienced "the big snow," which covered the ground from four to five inches. One county resident remembered that the corn crops "were up hand high," and had to be replanted.[6] No other losses were reported; the sun came out the next day and the snow melted.

The Kentucky Society, Sons of the Revolution, was instituted in Lexington on June 24, 1894, and incorporated January 26, 1895. The first officers were Leslie Combs, president; J. D. Livingston, vice-president; Wilbur R. Smith, secretary; Louis des Cognets, treasurer; Lucas Broadhead, registrar; H. B. McClellan, historian, and the Rev. W. S. Fulton, chaplain. There are about 125-135 members in the society whose ancestors had military service in the American Revolution. The annual banquet is held on April 19, to commemorate the Battle of Lexington, Mass.

On November 11, 1894, Charles C. Moore, self-styled "infidel" and "atheist," started a small, vitriolic newspaper called *The Blue Grass Blade,* which ran for several years in Lexington. Moore was sent to the federal prison at Columbus, Ohio, for sending obscene matter through the mails. While serving five months in prison he wrote his life story in a book titled *Behind the Bars, 31498,* published in Lexington in 1899. Editor Moore resided at his Quaker Acre farm on the Huffman Mill Pike, five and one-half miles north of the city.

The First Baptist Church organized the Fifth Street Baptist Church as a mission on January 15, 1892, at 239-241 East Fifth Street, opposite Maple Avenue. Worship was first held in a small frame chapel on the site. On November 18, 1894, a new brick church with tower was dedicated.

A front page of the Blue Grass Blade *(described above right).*

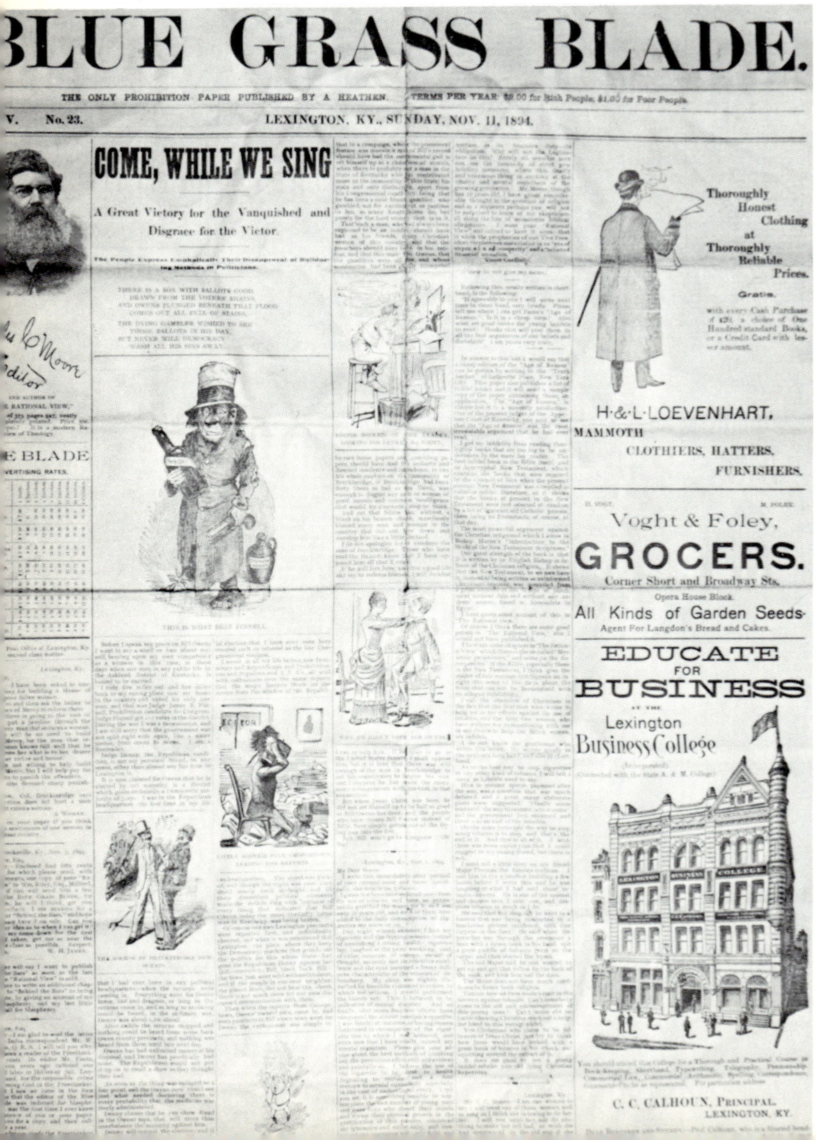

BLUE GRASS BLADE.

THE ONLY PROHIBITION PAPER PUBLISHED BY A HEATHEN. TERMS PER YEAR $2.00 for Rich People, $1.00 for Poor People.

V. No. 23. LEXINGTON, KY., SUNDAY, NOV. 11, 1894.

COME, WHILE WE SING

A Great Victory for the Vanquished and Disgrace for the Victor.

Thoroughly Honest Clothing at Thoroughly Reliable Prices.

H.&.L. LOEVENHART, MAMMOTH CLOTHIERS, HATTERS, FURNISHERS.

Voght & Foley, GROCERS. Corner Short and Broadway Sts.

All Kinds of Garden Seeds

EDUCATE FOR BUSINESS AT THE Lexington Business College

C. C. CALHOUN, PRINCIPAL. LEXINGTON, KY.

1895

On July 11, 1895, Lexington Lodge No. 89, Benevolent and Protective Order of Elks, was founded here, with William L. Simmonds, first exalted ruler. The lodge is in a thriving condition and meets in its building at 444 West Second Street.

Miss Ella M. Williams, daughter of Prof. Samuel M. Williams, former head of Sayre Female Institute, opened in 1895 a private school on the west side of North Upper Street 150 feet south of Second Street. In 1900 she moved her school to an ante-bellum residence at 355 North Broadway. About 125-140 boys and girls made up the student body, with five or six instructors. Miss Williams' school continued until around 1914; the building was razed in 1956 to make way for Transylvania's Forrer Hall which occupies the site.

The Episcopal Diocese of Lexington was established in 1895, with the Rt. Rev. Lewis W. Burton as the first bishop. This new diocese comprised the eastern half of Kentucky. Bishop Burton retired in 1928, and was succeeded by the Rt. Rev. H. P. Almon Abbott and he, in 1945, by the Rt. Rev. William R. Moody. The current and fourth bishop is the Rt. Rev. Addison Hosea, who was elected to the high office in 1970.

1896

Isaac Murphy, noted Negro jockey and three times rider of Kentucky Derby winners, was born in 1861, and died here on February 2, 1896. He was buried in the "No. 2 Cemetery" on East Seventh Street.[7] In April, 1967, his remains were removed to the Man o' War Park on the Huffman Mill Pike in this county, and a marker was erected to his memory.

Henry (Mud Dauber) Smith was hanged June 6, 1896, in the jail yard on East Short Street for the murder of a Mrs. Henderson, a tenant on the Walter S. Payne farm, on the Versailles Pike.

On Labor Day, September 7, 1896, a 100-mile bicycle race from Lexington to Covington was won by Cliff Nadaud of Covington in the record time of six hours, seven minutes and 56 seconds. C. Ora Updike and J. D. Jones of Lexington finished second and third in the race, which started in front of Thomas B. Dewhurst's bicycle shop on North Broadway, just above the Opera House, and terminated on Pike Street in Covington. First prize was a diamond-studded medal valued at $100.

During the year 1896 Lexington staged an exposition using the old Main Street Christian Church and the Navarre Cafe building on the opposite side of Main Street. A bridge was built across Main Street so that visitors to the exposition could visit the art gallery across the street without leaving the exposition "grounds."

The History of the Medical Department of Transylvania University by Dr. Robert Peter was published by the Filson Club, Louisville, 193 pages.

Transylvania University, Its Origin, Rise, Decline and Fall by Dr. Robert Peter and Johanna Peter was also published by The Filson Club, in a volume of 202 pages.

A view of the ruins of the courthouse after it was destroyed by fire on May 14, 1897 (described at left).

1897

On the morning of May 14, 1897, Lexington's fourth courthouse was destroyed by fire after an employee inadvertently dropped a match as he ascended to the belfry to wind the clock. Joel T. Hart's famous statue, "Woman Triumphant," was destroyed when the big bell in the tower fell down on it. A number of Matthew H. Jouett's paintings of county and state officials, papers, and law books were lost in the blaze, but most of the court records were saved. The loss was put at $55,000.

President William McKinley on July 10, 1897, made a brief stop at the C. & O. station about 11 P.M. while en route to Nashville. The train stopped for about 25 minutes and McKinley made a rear platform talk.

1898

The large, four-story brick Lexington Brewery, on the south side of East Main Street, opposite Deweese Street, was opened for business on January 30, 1898. It was demolished during the spring of 1941.

Several Spanish American War camps were established for soldiers in and around Lexington: Camp Collier at Tattersalls; Camp Miles on the Weil farm on the Versailles Pike; Camp Bradley in Woodland Park, and Camp Hobson on the Bryan Station Pike where the Fourth Kentucky was recruited. On August 12, 1898, the fighting in Cuba ended and Spain sought peace. Camp Hamilton was established five miles from town on the Bryan Station Pike and the Lexington & Eastern Railroad. It served as a mustering-out place for several thousand officers and soldiers from 11 states. The treaty with Spain was signed December 10, 1898, at Paris, France.

In 1898, the Independent Order of Odd Fellows established a widows' and orphans' home at the head of West Sixth Street in Lexington. A fine, four-story brick building with an octagonal tower was erected around 1898-1899, and this, with a two-story brick residence already on the grounds, constituted the Odd Fellows Widows and Orphans Home. A three-story brick building was erected in 1909, and some years later the two earlier buildings were replaced with a four-story brick boys' dormitory built in 1927. Both are still standing.

Lehman & Schmitt, of Cleveland, were architects for the present courthouse and the fourth on this site. Albert Howard and George Clark erected the structure during the years 1898-1900 at a cost of approximately $188,000.[8] The furniture, fixtures, and related work came to an additional $68,000. This courthouse is a large, three-story stone building with dome, weather vane and a clock on all four sides.

This year the football team of the Agricultural & Mechanical College of Kentucky (University of Kentucky) went through its eight game season undefeated, untied, and unscored on. The "Immortals of '98" were captained by Roscoe Severs and coached by William R. Bass of Cincinnati.[9]

J. Soule Smith, local attorney, published his book *Art Work of the Blue Grass Region of Kentucky.* The book is valuable for the fine pictures of houses and buildings no longer standing.

1899

The *Kentucky Historical and Genealogical Magazine* was started in Lexington by William H. Polk and W. C. Peay. Only two issues, May and June, 1899, were published. It was intended to be a monthly journal, with subscription $2.00 per year in advance.

1900

The first time an entire theater program was devoted to moving pictures in Lexington was January 25, 1900, when the 25 rounds of the "prize fight" between James J. Jeffries and Tom Sharkey was shown at the Lexington Opera House on North Broadway. Jeffries won the bout, which had been fought on November 3, 1899, at Coney Island, N. Y. At this time prize fights were favorite subjects for film makers.

On Sunday, October 6, 1900, the first commercially built automobile made its appearance on the streets of Lexington, advertising "Dr. Pierce's Golden Medical Discovery." The "gasoline motor machine" said the local press, was "a handsome four-wheeled affair," and "has a speed on level ground of 15 to 20 miles an hour." The machine was "put up" at Greenshaw & Morris livery stable and was to be in Lexington several days.[10] The paper did not state the make of the automobile.

Woodlands, the early home of Gen. George Trotter, Jr. and James Erwin, son-in-law of Henry Clay, was a large, two-story brick residence, with an octagonal room on each of the four corners. It stood in Woodland Park at the head of Park Avenue (present site of the municipal swimming pool). In 1866, the house and grounds were purchased by Kentucky University (Transylvania) for the establishment of the Agricultural & Mechanical College of Kentucky, which opened its doors that fall in the old mansion. The college remained here until it moved to its new location in 1882 on South Limestone Street. The old Trotter-Erwin residence was demolished around 1900-1902.

Lexington Banks of 1900-1905: Central National Bank, 201 West Short; Fayette National Bank, 167 West Main; First National Bank, 215 West Short; Lexington City National Bank, 259 West Main; National Exchange Bank, 255 West Main; Phoenix National Bank, 122 East Main; Second National Bank, 123 Cheapside; Third National Bank, 261 West Short, and Security Trust & Safety Vault Company, 271 West Short, corner of Mill.

During the years 1898-1900, people in the Bluegrass rebeled against the poor roads and the tolls charged for using them. Groups of "turnpike regulators" formed, and bands of armed men rode at night in vigilante fashion. Gate houses were burned and toll gatherers were horsewhipped. Some keepers were forced at gun point to cut the poles across the roads and burn them. The "war" had its telling effects. The counties then bought the turnpikes at reduced prices, and by 1900 practically all the turnpike roads in the Blue Grass were free.

The turnpikes and toll gates which radiated from Lexington in all directions were privately owned and operated, with toll gate houses five miles apart and one, a half-mile from the city limits. The toll rate was determined by the rate of wear on the road and travelers were taxed in proportion. Rates were: man on horseback, 5¢; horse and buggy, 10¢; two-horse carriage, 25¢; stage-coach with six passengers, 55¢; and hogs, sheep and cattle, 4¢ each. Preachers, doctors, school children and funeral processions were allowed to travel the roads without charge. Usually an Irish couple lived in the toll-gate house; the wife collected the fares while the husband kept the road in repair.

Prominent livery stables of the 1900-1915 period were: R. A. Downing, 230 West Vine; Jeff Harp, 134 North Limestone; Henry T. Horine, 115 South Spring; Z. T. Smiley, 527 West Short; T. B. Tracy, 146 Church; B. B. Wilson, 139-41 North Mill; Garrett D. Wilson, 118-20 East Main, and J. H. Wilson & Brother, 339-41 West Short. These stables were convenient places for country people to "put up" their buggies, surreys and carriages when they came to town. Livery stables also rented hacks and carriages for parties and weddings, as well as horses and buggies to traveling salesmen.

The Kentucky State Guard staff at Woodland Park.

Coolavin, the home of Judge Thomas Hickey, was built before 1800. This low, rambling, one-story brick house with wings, stood about 200 yards north of West Sixth Street between Price and Bellaire, neither of which had then been opened. The fine, ten room house was razed around 1900.

In 1899-1900, Thomas B. Dewhurst, a local mechanic and bicycle dealer, built the Dewabout, the first automobile to run on the streets of Lexington. This pioneer auto had a small four-horsepower, air-cooled engine mounted beneath the running gear of a buggy; it weighed about 350 pounds and had a cruising speed of fifteen miles an hour.[11]

The Dewabout (described above).

1901

Professor George W. Ranck, author of *History of Lexington* and other Kentucky books, was run over and killed while walking on the Louisville & Nashville Railroad tracks just below Tarr's Distillery in the west end of the city, on August 2, 1901. He was born in Louisville on February 13, 1841, and is buried in the Lexington Cemetery.

The seven-story McClelland Building at the northeast corner of Short and Upper streets were erected by Hendricks Brothers during the years 1900-1901. Originally the building was five stories; two more were added in 1905. This building now is the headquarters of the Central Bank & Trust Company.

Tom L. Walker's *History of the Lexington Post Office* was published by the E. D. Veach Company, Lexington.

1902

Judge James H. Mulligan of Maxwell Place read his famous poem, *In Kentucky,* on the evening of February 11, 1902, at a banquet at the Phoenix Hotel in honor of visiting members of the Kentucky legislature then in session.

Four interurban lines ran out of Lexington: to Georgetown, to Paris, to Nicholasville, and to Versailles and Frankfort, representing about 90-100 miles of trackage. These electric cars were about 50 feet long, ran on 640 volts d.c., with four-wheel trucks under the body, front and rear. The first car ran on the Lexington-Georgetown route May 25, 1902; the last line to Nicholasville was completed during 1909-1910. Electric current was furnished by the power house on Loudoun Avenue, and several substations between the towns. By 1920, the wooden cars were replaced with all-metal cars, operated by the motorman who collected the fares.

On September 6, 1902, President Theodore Roosevelt came through Lexington on a train en route to Chattanooga, and made a rear platform talk.

This year the numbering system for all down-town houses and buildings was changed. Limestone was substituted for Mill Street as the dividing line between the east and west, and the present numbering plan was adopted. Main Street continued to separate the northern and southern sections of the city, with all houses and buildings starting with No. 1.

1903

The Blue Grass Council No. 762, Knights of Columbus, was instituted in Lexington on April 26, 1903, with John M. Kelley, first grand knight. The lodge for Catholic men is now located at 1604 Versailles Road with a membership of 275. The national organization was established in 1882 at New Haven, Connecticut.

Earl Whitney and Claude O'Brien were hanged July 24, 1903, on a double scaffold in the jail yard on East Short Street for the murder of Addison B. Chinn, father of Asa Chinn, a local real estate dealer.[12]

On August 12, 1903, at the Elks Fair held at the Fair Grounds, two steam locomotives named Lexington and Louisville, were lined up facing each other 1,200 to 1,500 feet apart on a track laid in the center field. W. B. Curley, an I. C. engineer, and J. A. Wyatt, a C. & O. engineer, jumped off after opening the throttles, and the engines having gained considerable momentum ran together; both locomotives reared up and fell over on their sides, amid a great noise and hissing of steam. The staged wreck was the main feature of the 1903 fair.

In 1903, Professor Barton C. Hagerman purchased the large house at 437 West Second Street[13] and established Campbell-Hagerman College. Hagerman was president, assisted by G. P. Simmons associate president, with a faculty of 12. Degrees of A.B. and B.L. were conferred; in 1906 the enrollment totaled 150 young women from 16 states. A new brick building was erected on each side of the main building at Campbell-Hagerman College. Nearly 200 young ladies were graduated from this college before it closed in May, 1912.

1904

County Estates of the Bluegrass, by Thomas A. Knight and Nancy L. Greene, was published in Cleveland, Ohio. It is valuable for its pictures of houses and farms in the Central Kentucky area.

The participants in the first trial in the present courthouse paused for this photograph in February, 1900.

The replacement top of the Henry Clay monument statue and the sculptor's model. Chicagoan Charles J. Mulligan redid the statue after lightning struck the original in 1903.

At the northwest corner of Church and Mill streets stands the Y.W.C.A. Building, erected in 1904. This four-story brick building was built by the Y.M.C.A., on the site of the John Ready house. The men's organization vacated the building in August, 1932, and sold it six years later to the Y.W.C.A., which continues to occupy the property.

1905

James Bess, a contractor for carrying the U.S. mail, was arrested on March 10, 1903, two days after the body of a Mrs. Martin was found in a pond on East Sixth Street. Bess was hanged January 13, 1905, in the side yard of the Fayette County jail on East Short Street.

An early moving-picture show was Thomas A. Edison's *The Great Train Robbery,* which was shown in the spring of 1905 in the old frame auditorium in Woodland Park. This was a year or two before Lexington had any regular picture shows.

Founded in January, 1795, the Lexington Public Library had its offices on the Public Square, in Giron's Confectionery, and in the Transylvania Medical Hall at Church and Market streets. The cornerstone for the present two-story, cut-stone building was laid on June 8, 1903. Herman L. Rowe was the architect for the structure, which was opened to the public June 13, 1905. Cost of the building was $75,000 and $9,000 for the site. Andrew Carnegie contributed $60,000 towards the new library, which stands on Second Street between Mill and Market.

Rev. "Peter" Vinegar, a colorful Negro preacher, died in Lexington, July 9, 1905, "from the effects of age and extreme heat."[14] Some of his delightful sermon topics were: "A Damned Hot Day," "Watch dat Snake," and "Hell ain't but a mile from Lexington." He admonished his congregation: "Don't do as I do, *but do as I say do.*" He was said to have to have baptised more than 3,500 converts.

On September 7, 1904, the Security Trust & Safety Vault Company started construction of an eight-story brick building on the site of David A. Sayre's bank and its four-story building next door which it had recently sold. The present bank building at the northeast corner of Mill and Short streets, was completed on September 1, 1905. Two years later the bank's name was shortened to the Security Trust Company.

In September, 1905, the first Kentucky State Fair was held at the Fair Grounds in Lexington; it having been authorized by the Kentucky legislature and held under the auspicies of the Kentucky Live Stock Breeders Association. The next year the state fair was moved to Louisville.

The large, brick Woodland Park auditorium at the northeast corner of Kentucky Avenue and East High Street was completed by October 1, 1905. It replaced the old wooden auditorium near the center of the park. Many noted actors and shows have appeared in

A Sunday afternoon "baptizing" drew large crowds to this old pond near Bolivar Street.

Citizens comb the wreckage of a streetcar and a C&O passenger train which collided in May, 1907 (described on the following page). Miraculously, only the driver of the streetcar died.

Lexington physician Waller O. Bullock and his 1906 Franklin.

this brick auditorium; also there have been held high school commencements, Shrine ceremonials, boxing and wrestling matches. For some years past the building has been unoccupied.

1906

Fire on February 7, 1906, destroyed the Cincinnati Southern Railroad passenger station on South Broadway near Angliana Avenue.[15] This was a two-story frame building, and the loss was put at $20,000. The present two-story brick station was erected on the site.

In March, 1903, the congregation of the Upper Street Baptist Church changed its name to the Calvary Baptist Church and erected a handsome stone church with square tower at the southwest corner of Rodes Avenue and East High Street. Construction was begun on May 2, 1905, and the church was dedicated May 27, 1906, at a cost of $46,000. A fire on March 18, 1907, damaged several of the rooms and the west wall, but the building itself remained intact. Today the 69-year-old church is used as a recreational center for the new church on the opposite corner of Rodes Avenue. Dr. Thomas C. Ecton pastored this church for 39 years, from 1908 to 1947.

Early in July, 1888, Good Shepherd Church started as a mission of Christ Episcopal Church. A frame chapel with a Gothic window in the front gable was erected at 523 South Broadway and used for a number of years. In 1906, this building was taken down and rebuilt on East Maxwell Street, just west of the Maxwell School, corner of Woodland Avenue. Ten years later the mission became an independent parish.

On September 17, 1906, the Blue Grass Fair Association was formed by J. W. Porter and others to hold an annual fair to replace the state fair which had been moved to Louisville. The Blue Grass Fair continued to be held annually at the Fair Grounds through 1926 or 1927. Here also, Ringling Brothers and Barnum and Bailey Circus pitched their "big tops" near the center of the trotting track. The Kentucky Trotting Horse Breeders Association holds its annual spring and fall meets here. Currently and for some years past, the Fair Grounds have been used by the Plug Horse Derby, the Junior League Horse Show, the Shrine Circus and other forms of entertainment, as well as the annual Lions Club Fair.

The first movie theater in Lexington was the Theatorium, located at 111-113 Cheapside, which opened late in 1905 or early in 1906. Others followed the next year or two; The Princess, 237 West Main Street; Blue Grass Theater, 404 West Main; Phoenix Theater, 116 East Main; Colonial Theater, 224 West Main, and the Star Theater, 108 North Upper Street. The Strand Theater at 153 East Main began showing pictures around 1910.

Charles Bohmer of Virginia opened the first "loose-leaf" tobacco warehouse in Lexington and this system of selling developed steadily. Lexington took its place as the major burley auction market, replacing Louisville as the sales center. Today, there are about thirty loose-leaf warehouses in the city, selling tobacco grown all over Central and Eastern Kentucky.

1907

On January 1, 1907, a group of Lexington businessmen organized the Lexington Country Club and purchased acreage on the east side of the Maysville Pike, about three miles from town. They built a large, frame clubhouse. This building burned October 19, 1925, and was replaced with the present one.

In March, 1907, the old Upper Street Baptist Church (built in 1877) at the southwest corner of Church and Upper streets was remodeled by Milton J. Davis, who opened the Lyric Theater in the building.[16] Several years later a new front was put on the church building, and in 1912 it became the main office and exchange for the Fayette Home Telephone Company.

Union Station, the new passenger station, was opened for business on April 4, 1907. It was built (1904-1907) and used jointly by the C. & O., L. & E., and L. & N. railroads. Stanford White of New York was the architect for the station, which stood on the south side of East Main Street west of the present Harrison Avenue Viaduct. After the L. & N. Railroad discontinued its passenger service, the Union Station was torn down in March, 1960. Several years later, the C. & O. Railroad built a small passenger station at 1008 Delaware Avenue and used it until May, 1971, when its crack train the George Washington was taken off the run.

About mid-morning May 9, 1907, a city streetcar and an eastbound C. & O. passenger train were involved in a wreck at Water Street and South Broadway. Brakes failed the streetcar as it descended the South Broadway hill and it crashed into the baggage car of the train, turning it over on its side. George Wells, the motorman, was killed and all twenty passengers on the streetcar were injured; one person on the train was slightly hurt.[17]

Lexington's first vaudeville theater was the Hippodrome at 325 West Main Street which opened on November 25, 1907. The Majestic at 108 North Upper Street was the second; it opened December 2, 1907. Six years later the Hippodrome was changed to the Ada Meade Theater, in honor of Miss Ada Meade Saffarans, a Lexington girl and musical comedy star. The "Hipp" as it came to be known, offered vaudeville and motion pictures, but in later years showed only motion pictures. The theater was torn down in 1954 to make way for Purcell's parking lot.

This lake in Woodland Park was drained after a child drowned there. Today softball games are played on a diamond built in the lake's depression.

The Blue Grass League, a professional baseball league, operated in Central Kentucky from about 1907 through 1928. Lexington's ball park was located on the west side of North Broadway between Seventh Street and the Belt Line Railroad (later Transylvania's football field). Original league members were Lexington, Paris, Winchester, Frankfort, Nicholasville, Versailles, and Mt. Sterling. Later, at various times, the league included Shelbyville, Harrodsburg, Danville, Georgetown, Cynthiana, and Maysville. The Blue Grass League produced some noted players including Jimmy Viox, Fred Toney and Casey Stengel.

Park Methodist Church at the northwest corner of East High Street and Clay avenue was completed around 1907, with the Rev. O. B. Crockett its pastor. The church currently has a membership of over 1,000.

This year the Good Samaritan Hospital, which had its inception in the old Protestant Infirmary on East Short Street, was moved to its present location on South Limestone Street just south of Maxwell. The hospital in 1925 was put under the auspicies of the Southern Methodist Church. In 1930, the Mary A. Ott Memorial building was added to the front of the hospital's main entrance.

1908

The cornerstone of the present building was laid on January 13, 1908, and the First Methodist Church was dedicated January 10, 1909, at 214 West High Street, between Upper and Mill streets.[18] For many years this was the only Methodist church in Lexington, formerly known as the Hill Street Methodist Church and currently named the First United Methodist Church.

An act passed by the Kentucky legislature March 16, 1908, changed the name of the Agricultural & Mechanical College of Kentucky to State University, Lexington, Kentucky — the name of the city and state being a part of the corporate title. By the same act, Transylvania on the opposite side of town, which had been known as Kentucky University since 1865, reverted to its pioneer name Transylvania University.

St. John's Academy, a parochial school for boys, established in 1854, in the rear of St. Peter's Catholic Church on North Limestone, was merged in 1902 with St. Paul's School. In April, 1908, the old two-story brick building, facing on Walnut Street, was torn down.[19]

Oleika Temple of the Ancient Arabic Order Nobles of the Mystic Shrine was chartered in Lexington, July 15, 1908, with William J. Cardwell appointed first potentate. John G. Cramer was the first elected potentate in 1909. Oleika's current membership is well over 3,000.

On the night of September 22, 1908, Willis E. Smith, a freshman at State University mysteriously disappeared from the campus. All sorts of wild stories were circulated around town; foul play was suspected, possibly from hazing by upper classmen. After a week's investigation failed to locate Smith's body, the case became a statewide sensation. Three months later Smith turned up alive at his home in Owensboro and told a hair-raising story of how he had been kidnapped, drugged, and transported in a railway freight car to Wisconsin and held captive in a cave. The strange disappearance of Willis E. Smith became a matter of much conjecture; the errant freshman never returned to U.K. to complete his studies.

Around 1904-05, tobacco was bringing only 5 to 6 cents a pound. Protective associations were formed and attempted to force the large national companies to pay a better price for the tobacco by persuading farmers to withhold their crops from the market. Those who refused were dubbed "hill-billies." Activities of the association members took on the guise of the Ku Klux Klan, whipping and shooting the hillbillies, and scraping tobacco beds. The Burley Tobacco Society was formed in 1906 in the Bluegrass, where some of the night-riding activity was seen. Several barns were burned and Lexington warehouses were guarded by soldiers of the National Guard. The night-rider war ended in 1908, and peace was restored to Central and Western Kentucky.

St. John's Academy (described below left).

Morton High School (described below).

The Knights of Pythias dedicated their new state widows and orphans home here in 1908, at which time 65 subordinate lodges were represented and about 2,500 persons witnessed the ceremonies. This building stood several hundred yards east of the junction of Clay's Mill Road and the Harrodsburg Pike, near the antebellum residence of architect John McMurtry, known as The Elms.

1909

A new Morton High School at the southeast corner of Walnut and Short streets, replaced the old Morton School No. 1, which had been built in 1849. The cornerstone of the new four-story red brick building was laid on February 15, 1909, and the school was completed the next year at a cost of $53,795. Herman L. Rowe & Company were architects; Combs Lumber Company the general contractors. The school was closed in 1937 and the building was demolished during the summer of 1940.

The Lexington automobile was manufactured in this city during the years 1909 to 1910. The plant then moved to Connersville, Indiana, and the car's name was changed to the Lexington Minute-Man Six. The factory here was on the south side of West Main Street where the Savage Lumber Company is located at the West Main Viaduct and the Southern Railroad tracks.

Notes

1. *Lexington Morning Transcript*, April 23, 1891.
2. *Ibid.*, June 2, 1892.
3. *Kentucky Leader*, August 8, 1893.
4. *Lexington Morning Transcript*, November 26, 1893.
5. *Kentucky Leader*, April 30, 1893.
6. *Lexington Herald*, April 30, 1893.
7. *Ibid.*, May 5, 1961.
8. Coleman, *The Court Houses of Lexington*, p. 32.
9. *The Courier-Journal*, September 17, 1933.
10. *Lexington Leader*, October 7, 1900.
11. Letter from Dewhurst to the author, October 11, 1932.
12. *Lexington Morning Democrat*, July 25, 1903.
13. The Thomas January house built in the early 1800s.
14. *Frankfort Roundabout*, July 22, 1905.
15. *Lexington Herald*, February 8, 1906.
16. *Ibid.*, March 24, 1907.
17. *Ibid.*, May 10, 1907.
18. *Ibid.*, January 14, 1908.
19. *Lexington Morning Herald*, April 26, 1908.

1910-1929

An Era of War, Fires, Hangings and Prohibition

Soon after Lexington dedicated the equestrian statue of Civil War hero John Hunt Morgan, the city was involved in preparations for World War I. Despite prohibition, times were none too quiet in the Blue Grass. Before Lexington's last hanging in 1926, four had occurred in the period. Public emotion ran so high over a 1920 incident that military rule had to be declared with army troops called from Camp Knox.

1910

Professor James K. Patterson was appointed head of the Agricultural & Mechanical College of Kentucky in 1869. He served in that capacity until he resigned in 1910 after the longest term of any college president in America. He was called "He Pat" by the college boys and his brother, Walter Patterson, was dubbed "She Pat," since he had once been assistant "matron" of the girls' dormitory. The president's son, William Andrew, was nicknamed "It Pat," and the University of Kentucky's school of diplomacy was named for him in accordance with a bequest from James K. Patterson.

1911

The transfer station, known as the "waiting center," stood in the center of West Main Street opposite Cheapside, and was constructed around 1891-1892 from an old street car. Here all city and interurban passengers waited, bought tickets and boarded the cars. The station was declared a public nuisance by the grand jury and was razed on June 23, 1911.[1]

Ten thousand persons witnessed the unveiling of the equestrian statue of General John Hunt Morgan on October 18, 1911 on the courthouse lawn. General Basil W. Duke, Morgan's brother-in-law, had charge of the ceremonies. The statue was sculptured by Pompeo Coppini, of San Antonio, Texas, at a cost of $15,000. Local attorney Hogan Yancey posed as the model for the Confederate general, who is buried in the Lexington Cemetery. The inscription on the monument reads: "General John Hunt Morgan and his Men."

President William H. Taft passed through Lexington on November 8, 1911, on a special train which stopped briefly, but he did not make an appearance.[2]

In the fall of 1911, the Hipp Annex was opened on the west side of the Hippodrome, which offered a moving-picture show plus spotlight singers, for the sum of five cents.

In 1911, the Third National Bank and the Phoenix National Bank were consolidated forming the Phoenix & Third National Bank. This bank later acquired the assets of the Lexington Banking & Trust Company.

Mary Desha, one of the founders of the National Society, Daughters of the American Revolution, and granddaughter of Governor Joseph Desha, was born in Lexington in 1850. She taught in the Lexington public school from 1875 to 1885. Miss Desha died in Washington, D. C. in 1911 and is buried in the Lexington Cemetery.

1912

The Orpheum Theater at the southeast corner of Main and Limestone, a popular motion-picture house, opened on April 20, 1912, and ran for a number of years. J. H. Stamper, Jr., was owner and manager.[3] The Orpheum sign can be seen in the picture of Main Street on the facing page.

Lexingtonians flooded bleachers, the courthouse yard, and Main and Upper streets to attend the unveiling of the statue of Gen. John Hunt Morgan astride his horse, Black Bess. The crowd was estimated to be over 10,000.

About midnight, October 30, 1912, a fire occurred in the office of Dean F. Paul Anderson in Mechanical Hall at State University which destroyed books, records and furniture; the total loss was estimated at $3,000.[4] Many persons believed the fire was started to destroy records of the athletic association kept in Anderson's office, for at the time, the school was faced with suspension from the Southern Intercollegiate Athletic Association on the ground that it had played ineligible men on its football teams.

In November, 1912, the Fayette Home Telephone Company, with quarters in the remodeled Upper Street Baptist Church at Upper and Church, acquired the assets of the East Tennessee & Cumberland Telephone companies, thus ending the dual telephone system which had been in effect in Lexington and Fayette County for ten or twelve years.

The Bank of Commerce was organized December 19, 1911, and opened for business in January, 1912, in a small building at 111 East Main Street, several doors east of Limestone. Starting capital was $100,000, with Irwin W. Mantle, president, and Fred G. Stiltz, cashier. The bank's main office now is in a new two-story brick building at 318 East Main Street opposite Deweese.

Lexington Banks 1912-1917: Bank of Commerce, 111 East Main; Fayette National Bank, 167 West Main; First National Bank, 215 West Short; Lexington Banking & Trust Company, 249 West Short; Lexington City National Bank, 271 West Main; Phoenix & Third National Bank, 123-25 West Main; Second National Bank, 123 Cheapside; Security Trust Company, corner of Mill and Short; Union Bank & Trust Company, 164 West Main, and Title Guaranty & Trust Company, 201-03 West Short Street.

The State University basketball team of 1912 was champion of Kentucky and unofficial champion of the South. Two of the outstanding players on the team were Brinkley Barnett and Derrell Hart.

1913

James Ben Ali Haggin, a copper tycoon, erected the Ben Ali Theater on the north side of Main Street opposite the Phoenix Hotel. It opened on September 23, 1913. The stage was said to have been one of the finest in the South, with a $1,500 velvet curtain. The theater had a seating capacity of 1,507 persons, with a large balcony and twelve boxes.

John Wilson Townsend's two-volume work, *Kentucky in American Letters,* was published by the Torch Press, Cedar Rapids, Iowa.

1914

The Fayette National Bank erected a 15-story building at the northeast corner of Main and Upper streets during the period 1913-1914. McKein, Meade and White, New York architects, designed the "skyscraper," which was erected by the George A. Fuller Company of Knoxville, Tenn. The building was opened to the public on January 30, 1914. The old three-story brick Fayette National Bank, erected in 1871-72, had been razed to make way for the new structure, which is now the main office of the First Security National Bank & Trust Company.

1915

The First Baptist Church, a large and handsome building of Bedford Indiana limestone, standing on the north side of West Main Street opposite Patterson and west of Felix Street, had its cornerstone laid October 6, 1913, and was dedicated June 3, 1915, by the Rev. J. W. Porter.[5] This church replaced the old brick church built in 1868 on the same site which had faced on West Short Street. During the construction of this church, the grave of John Bradford, Kentucky's first printer and newspaperman, was discovered under the west wall of the structure. The grave was left undisturbed.

The Lexington Rotary Club, the second in Kentucky, was established here on June 23, 1915, with 21 charter members. George T. Graves was elected the first president. This was the first civic club established in Lexington.

Opposite the Lexington Opera House at 144-46 North Broadway stands the three-story red brick Masonic Temple, erected at a cost of $40,000 and dedicated December 29, 1915. Frank L. Smith was the architect and J. T. Jackson Lumber Company, general contractors. Lexington Lodge No. 1 and Devotion Lodge No. 160 meet in the temple, together with all branches of the York Rite and two Eastern Star bodies.

Belfast, the handsome, two-story brick residence of David Megowan, was built before 1800 and razed in 1915. It stood on the north side of East Main Street slightly west of the present-day North Eastern Avenue, formerly called Megowan Street.

1916

On the morning of January 11, 1916, fire gutted the Ben Ali Theater on East Main Street. Loss to the building and equipment was more than $100,000.[6] In later years the theater was converted into a moving-picture house. The last show was on September 9, 1964, when the picture "A Home Is Not a House," was shown. The Ben Ali building was demolished in 1965, and a parking garage was erected on the site.

Located at the southwest corner of Second and Broadway, the Broadway Christian Church, with circular brick tower, burned on February 27, 1916. An overheated flue or defective wiring caused the fire which smoldered in the attic for two hours during the morning service. It broke out at 1:35 P.M., and two hours later the structure was in ruins. The loss was estimated at $50,000.[7]

On March 16, 1916, State University, Lexington, Kentucky, was changed to its present name, the University of Kentucky. The state institution had been organized in February, 1865, as the Agricultural & Mechanical College of Kentucky.

E. H. WARFIELD. J. C. ANDERSON.

WARFIELD & CO.

AND DEALERS IN

PURE COPPER WHISKY,

CHEAPSIDE, LEXINGTON, KY.

WE GUARANTEE ALL WHISKY SOLD BY US PURE AND FREE FROM ADULTERATION.

ORDERS SOLICITED.

GAZETTE PR.

The John Bradford Historical Society was formed in Lexington on May 4, 1916, to honor the first printer in the West and "to collect and preserve historical materials relating to Lexington and the state." Forty to fifty prominent citizens, including Judge Samuel M. Wilson, were charter members. The society ceased to function after 1960.

President Woodrow Wilson was in Lexington September 4, 1916, en route to and from the dedication of the Lincoln Memorial near Hodgenville, which he accepted on behalf of the United States. He was here about three A.M., and again at 8:55 P.M., on a special train out of Washington.

1917

On Monday morning, May 21, 1917, flames swept the greater part of the block bounded by Church, Short, Limestone and Upper streets. The five-story, brick Merrick (I.O.O.F.) Lodge building (erected in 1893) at the northwest corner of Short and Limestone burned, together with several livery stables, business houses and residences.[8]

Sparks from the Merrick Lodge fire landed in the tower of the large, brick Second Presbyterian Church on Market near Second, and totally destroyed it. The loss was put at $50,000. It had been erected in 1846-47, for $18,000. The Williams Apartments on Market Street now occupy the site.

With the advent of World War I in 1917, all able-bodied male students at the University of Kentucky were enrolled in four military organizations. The Students Army Training Corps was housed in several two-story wooden barracks erected by the War Department at the southwest corner of Rose and Winslow (now Euclid) streets. This was Camp Buell, which occupied eight to ten acres. Students continued their classes, drilled an hour or two each day and lived in the company barracks. The camp was named for Union General Don Carlos Buell.

At the outbreak of World War I in 1917, Camp Stanley was established on the 245-acre farm of Garrett W. Wilson (Lansing Farm) on the north side of the Versailles Pike west of Hamilton Park. Three hundred "box barracks" were erected. The 250-acre Weil farm on the Versailles Pike also was rented by the government at $6,000 per annum and used as a camp. Lexington was the mobilization point for all Kentucky troops and others from out of the state.

1918

On January 20, 1918, fire destroyed the Good Shepherd Episcopal Church on the south side of East Maxwell Street next door to the Maxwell School. Frozen fire hydrants and sub-zero weather hindered the fire fighters and the frame structure was a total loss.[9] The church sued the city for low water pressure; but no verdict was reached. Services for the next several years were held in the Maxwell School.

Samuel Woodson Price, noted Kentucky portrait painter, was born August 5, 1828, at Sugar Grove near Nicholasville. In 1849 he painted an oil portrait of William "King" Solomon, which launched him on his art career. Price painted many portraits of prominent Kentuckians. He served as a Union general in the Civil War, was seriously wounded at the battle of Kennesaw Mountain, was military commandant of Lexington during 1864-65, and postmaster, 1869-72. General Price died in St. Louis on January 22, 1918, and was buried in the Arlington National Cemetery.

Dr. David Barrow, a local surgeon, organized the Good Samaritan Base Hospital Unit No. 40, which was mobilized February 24, 1918, with a total of 223 enlisted personnel, 100 nurses and 48 medical officers. The unit trained at Camp Taylor. It left on July 5, 1918 for England aboard the British ship Scotian. The Barrow unit consisted largely of local men and women; it was mustered out of service in April, 1919.

1919

The National Prohibition Act was passed by the sixty-fifth Congress on January 29, 1919, to become effective one year after ratification by three-fourths of the states. The Volstead Act prohibited the manufacture, transportation, and sale of intoxicating liquors and beers. Before it went into effect, January 16, 1920, hundreds of Lexington citizens crowded into the bars and saloons to lay in a goodly supply of liquor and beer.

After their church burned in 1916, the congregation of Broadway Christian Church erected the present brick building on the same site, at the southwest corner of Broadway and Second. Richards, McCarty & Rulford, of Columbus, Ohio, designed the new edifice, which cost $135,000 and was dedicated on May 4, 1919, by George L. Sniverly.

1920

On February 9, 1920, Will Lockett, a Negro, was tried for the assault and murder five days earlier of ten-year-old Geneva Hardman at South Elkhorn. A mob formed in front of the courthouse before nine o'clock with the avowed intention of taking the prisoner from the courtroom and hanging him. Adjutant General James M. Deweese with 97 members of the State Guards had been brought in to preserve order. As the mob rushed up the front steps of the courthouse, soldiers and deputies inside the building fired; six men were killed and 50-odd wounded. Gen. Francis C. Marshall with several companies of the Rainbow Division of the United States Army were rushed by train from Camp Knox and put the city under military rule. This quickly ended the mob action. Lockett died in the electric chair at Eddyville Prison March 11, 1920.

1921

On January 11, 1921, a spectacular fire occurred in several stores on the south side of West Main Street between Mill and Broadway. The buildings damaged by the blaze were the Wolf Wile Company, J. D. Purcell Company, Kaufman-Straus Clothing Company and the Peerless store. Estimates of the damage ranged from $690,000 to $800,000.

On July 9, 1921, the seven-day Redpath Chautauqua opened in a big tent on the lot (site old Henry Clay High School) at the northeast corner of Main Street and Walton Avenue. A play, "The Man from Home," and Shakespeare's "As You Like It" were among the attractions, which also included band music, vocalists, lectures, a program of magic and numerous others.

Immanuel Baptist Church, the outgrowth of the Tabernacle Baptist Church on South Upper Street, moved to the northwest corner of Woodland Avenue and East High Street and dedicated a new edifice on July 31, 1921. The building is currently known as the Woodland Avenue Baptist Church.

The Lafayette Hotel was built during the period 1920-21, and opened for business on December 1, 1921. The $1,300,000 structure was designed by Chris Weber, Cincinnati, and built by the Mason & Hanger Company. The twelve-story building was the latest in hotel design, and stands on the south side of East Main Street opposite Walnut. In 1960, the building was sold to the Kentucky Central Insurance Company and the hotel closed in February, 1963. The building is currently used as the insurance company offices.

The first concrete highway in Kentucky was built in 1921 by the Louis des Cognets Company, a seven-mile stretch on the Lexington-Winchester Pike in Fayette County. Total cost of the construction was $192,182.38, which was paid by the federal and state governments.[10]

On a set Monday in each month the court day sales and gatherings were held on Cheapside, where horses, mules, cows and

Two views of the Lockett mob (described above).

A photograph of one of the last court days on Cheapside.

calves were sold, together with a nondescript assortment of old furniture, cooking stoves, axe handles, buggy harness, farming implements, home-made baskets, sugar-cane "sweeting," and molasses by the gallon. Also in the ante-bellum days slave sales were held here. After many years the custom of holding court day sales on Cheapside was declared a public nuisance and it was legally abolished on October 26, 1921. The space was filled in, trees planted and the public square became a city park.

1922

On April 8, 1922, the "Blue Devils" of Lexington High School won the national championship by defeating Mt. Vernon, Ohio, in the finals by the score of 44 to 28. Members of the team were Burgess Carey, Len Tracy, Will Milward III, Lowell Underwood and Jimmy McFarland. Other members of the Blue Devils who saw action were Foster Helm, J. L. Darnaby and E. J. Davis. The championship game was played at the University of Chicago.

The Kentucky Theater, built on the site of H. G. Smitha's livery stable, at 214 East Main Street, several doors east of the Lafayette Hotel, was opened as a motion picture house in 1922. Four years later, the first "talking pictures" in Lexington were shown here. This innovation was the Vitaphone. A phonograph record was synchronized to play with the film strip, or at least it was supposed to.

1923

The Felix Memorial Baptist Church, which in 1916 had changed its name from the Fifth Street Baptist Church, erected a fine, two-story yellow brick church on the site at 239-41 East Fifth Street. The church has two entrances and six pilasters on the front of the building.

1924

The contract for the concrete stadium at the University of Kentucky was awarded May 1, 1924, to local contractor Louis des Cognets & Company for $116,520 for construction of six sections of the stadium, the playing field, and the dressing-room facilities under the stands. The U. K. Wildcats and Centre College played the first game in the stadium on October 20, 1924. This structure stands on the south side of Euclid Avenue near Rose Street.

After their fine Second Presbyterian Church on Market Street burned in 1917, the Presbyterians (U.S.A.) erected their present stone building at 460 East Main Street at Ransom Avenue. Cost of the new structure was approximately $250,000. It was dedicated on December 21, 1924.

1925

James Lane Allen, noted author, novelist, and short-story writer, was born near Lexington on December 21, 1849, and died in New York City on February 18, 1925. He is buried in the Lexington Cemetery where the John Bradford Historical Society on Nov. 19, 1950 erected a suitable monument to his memory. Allen was the author of such well-known books as the *Flute and Violin, A Kentucky Cardinal, The Choir Invisible, The Blue Grass Region of Kentucky,* and *The Reign of Law.*

On June 4, 5, and 6, 1925, Lexington celebrated its one hundred and fiftieth anniversary with a "Grand Historical Pageant" held in the University of Kentucky stadium. Fifteen hundred men, women, and children had parts in the ten episodes, which included Lafayette's visit to Lexington, raiding with General Morgan, the siege of Bryan's Station, pioneer railway (Lex. & Ohio) of the West, and the inauguration of Isaac Shelby. Costumes were rented from a Philadelphia house. J. C. Burton, of Monticello, Ky., drove his father's four-horse stage coach to Lexington to appear in the pageant, the overall cost of which was put at $20,000.

Blue Grass Park, originally known as the Belt Line Park, was owned and operated by the Kentucky Traction & Terminal Company. Interurban cars were run from Lexington on the hour. The park, incorporated June 10, 1909, was "Lexington's greatest amusement park and fresh air resort," and was located six miles from town on the north side of the Versailles Pike immediately west of the South Elkhorn Baptist Church and covered about 20 acres. All kinds of amusements were enjoyed, including roller-coaster rides, dancing, swimming, and boating on the creek which ran through the grounds. The park closed in June-July, 1925,[11] after Joyland Park on the Paris Pike had been opened.

The cornerstone for the Good Shepherd Episcopal Church at the west corner of Bell Court and East Main Street, was laid on August 25, 1925, by Bishop Lewis W. Burton. The church was formally opened for divine worship on November 15, 1926. The old bell from the Central Fire Station on West Short Street was put in the tower of this fine stone meeting house.

On July 3, 1924, Ray Ross, a 25-year-old Negro attacked and raped Willie Mae Young, a nine-year-old Negro girl, in a vacant house on North Limestone. Ross was convicted in the Fayette Circuit Court on October 16, 1924. After numerous legal delays, Ross was hanged from a scaffold in the jail yard on East Short Street, at 4:23 A.M., August 28, 1925. The local press said: "A very large crowd gathered to watch the execution and cheered loudly when he was hung."[12]

One of the most spectacular fires in Lexington history occurred at Dick Webb's Mammoth Garage on East Main Street on the night of August 29, 1925. A crowd of three to four thousand persons watched the fire which caused an estimated damage of $225,000. In the blaze 32 new automobiles were reported lost.

Wild Life in Kentucky, by William D. Funkhouser, was published by the Kentucky Geological Survey, 386 pages, Frankfort.

On the evening of December 26, 1925, William Nelson Fant, son of a wealthy Flemingsburg banker and some 10 or 12 men were playing cards in an upper room of the Henry Clay Hotel, at 116 West Main Street between the Graves, Cox store and Limestone Street. Two men, Roger Brannon and R. C. Davis, entered the room and proceeded to rob each man separately. Fant objected to giving up his diamond ring, a struggle ensued and he was shot and killed. Both of the robbers were given the death sentence.

1926

On the night of January 19, 1926, Clarence Bryant, his daughter Ethel and son Wilbur were shot to death by Ed Harris, a Negro, in a tenant house on the Coldstream Farm on the Newtown Pike. Mrs. Maggie Bryant, the wife, survived though badly injured and beaten.[13] On the day of Harris' trial (Feb. 2) 1,000 National Guardsmen were on duty in Lexington and the city was under military rule. Harris was convicted and hanged March 5, 1926, in the side yard of the county jail on East Short Street. This was the last hanging in Fayette County.

The Shriners Crippled Children Hospital, was first opened on

A 1926 view of two interurban and city streetcars and a new motor bus on West Main Street.

April 11, 1926, in a large, two-story frame residence at the southwest corner of Maxwell and Harrison Avenue. The hospital continued in that location until the new fifty-bed unit was built and dedicated on May 29, 1955, at 1900 Richmond Road on a 28.3 acre tract of land. John T. Gillig was the architect and Robert D. Short the contractor. The total cost of the land, building, and equipment was put at $1,134,000. The Shriners Hospital, across from the Idle Hour Country Club, is a charitable institution for children up to sixteen years of age, regardless of race, color, or creed.

Judge Samuel M. Wilson, a noted lawyer and Kentucky historian, sponsored the Cakes & Ale Club which met annually in his home at 423 Fayette Park. The first meeting was held on February 1, 1926, and thereafter around Washington's birthday. Forty-five to fifty men were invited to the party each year, enjoying a five-course dinner served by a caterer. Invitations were printed in quaint Old English. Local, state and nationally known authors, historians and bibliophiles shared the ambiance of the occasion. The club met for about 20 years.[14]

1927

Opened in the Ben Ali Theater on April 4, 1927, by the Rev. J. Archer Gray, a "deposed" minister from Maxwell Presbyterian Church, Everybody's Church was non-denominational in scope. This church later moved to the Centennary Methodist Church building at Broadway and Church streets, and the congregation took title to the property on June 6, 1958. Today the church is known as the First Community Church of Lexington.

The Lexington Cadillac Garage, at the northeast corner of Main and Deweese streets, was destroyed by fire on December 20, 1927. A number of new and used cars were lost in the blaze, which caused damage of about $65,000.

1928

On June 29, 1928, Lexington experienced a flood of considerable portions; water rose in front of the Phoenix Hotel to a depth of two to three feet. The Town Branch had overflowed and basements along Main Street were filled with water. Damage was estimated to run into the thousands of dollars.

Ancient Life in Kentucky, by William D. Funkhouser and William S. Webb, was published by the Kentucky Geological Survey, 349 pages, Frankfort, Ky.

The ante-bellum Davenport house on the east side of Walnut Street, facing Barr Street, was razed late in 1926 and the cornerstone for the present City Hall was laid on December 5, 1927. Architects for the building which was completed in 1928, were Leon K. Frankel and John J. Curtis. The Davenport residence was a handsome, two-story brick, with pilasters on the front corners and two in the center behind the one-story porch. It stood just north of Central Christian Church.

1929

On the night of February 11, 1929, St. Joseph's Hospital on West Second Street was badly damaged by fire. The third and fourth floors were gutted, but every patient was carried from the building and there were no fatalities. Twenty-five hose lines were run into the building and 560,000 gallons of water used to quench the fire. Loss was estimated at $100,000.[15] The hospital was rebuilt, and remained on this site until 1959.

On March 4, 1929, the First & City National Bank and the Phoenix National Bank were consolidated under the name of First National Bank & Trust Company, with William H. Courtney as head of the organization. On April 27, 1931, the newly organized bank assumed control of the Fayette National Bank and moved into its fifteen-story building at the northeast corner of Main and Upper streets.

The clubhouse of the Lexington Country Club burned during the night of October 19, 1925. It was replaced by the present facility.

Waters were receding in this picture of the 1928 flood (described at left), but automobiles in front of Union Station and the Hotel Layfayette were still axle-deep in water. Town Branch which flows beneath Vine Street was unable to carry off the water from this June deluge.

The final "tap out" from the Central Fire Station on the south side of West Short Street between Limestone and Upper, was on June 7, 1929. The department left the old station, erected in 1888, and moved to its present quarters in a new two-story yellow brick building on the north side of East Third Street, 100 feet east of Walnut and next to the old Catholic cemetery. The new Central Fire Station was built in 1929 by Skinner Brothers at a cost of $40,000.

The cornerstone for the new cut-stone church on the north side of Barr Street, St. Peter's Catholic Church, was laid on November 27, 1927.[16] The church was dedicated by the Most Rev. Francis W. Howard on April 7, 1929. Total cost of the church was around $200,000. It stands on the site of Judge Watts Parker's house at 153 Barr Street.

William H. Townsend's *Lincoln and His Wife's Home Town* was published in 1929. Later, in 1955, it was republished in an expanded edition by the University of Kentucky Press under the title, *Lincoln and the Bluegrass.*

Central Fire Station (described above).

Notes

1. *Lexington Leader,* June 21, 1961.
2. *Ibid.,* April 20, 1954.
3. *Ibid.,* April 20, 1912.
4. *Ibid.,* November 3, 1912.
5. *Lexington Herald,* June 3, 1915.
6. *Ibid.,* January 12, 1916.
7. *Ibid.,* February 28, 1916.
8. *Lexington Leader,* May 21, 1917.
9. *Lexington Herald,* May 5, 1920.
10. *The Courier-Journal,* December 18, 1937.
11. *Lexington Leader,* June 19, 1925.
12. *Ibid.,* August 28, 1925.
13. *Lexington Herald-Leader,* January 20, 1926.
14. Recollections of the author.
15. *Lexington Herald,* February 12, 1929.
16. *Ibid.,* November 27, 1927.

1930-1949

Some Old Traditions Die While New Ones Are Born

This recent era saw the end of the interurban following a strike, the closing of the Kentucky Association track, the end of prohibition, and the death of Man o'War. Yet the beginning of downtown parking meters, night football, the Junior League horse show, and the integration of the University of Kentucky were events of the two decades that now seem to have always been a part of Lexington.

1930

The University of Kentucky played its first night football game, possibly the first in the South, in McLean Stadium on Euclid Avenue, against the University of the South (Sewanee) in Lexington on October 4, 1930. The Wildcats won by the score of 37 to 0.

St. Peter's Catholic Church, the old church (built 1836-37) on the east side of North Limestone a few doors south of Third Street, was torn down in the fall of 1930. MacCabe in his 1838 city directory, described it as "a neat and spacious edifice, measuring, including the sanctuary, 90 by 50 feet." The church had a bell tower and steeple. A biblical inscription over the front door read: "Thou art Peter and upon this rock I will build my church, and the gates of hell shall not prevail against it." The venerable meetinghouse had been replaced the year before with the new stone church on Barr Street.

In the 1930s and 1940s the following banks were in operation: Bank of Commerce, 269 West Main; Commonwealth Bank & Trust Company, Short and Limestone; Citizens Bank & Trust Company, 201-03 West Short; First National Bank & Trust Company, 167 West Main; Kentucky Joint Stock Land Bank, 271 West Short; Second National Bank, 123 Cheapside; Security Trust Company, 271 West Short; and the Union Bank & Trust Company, 215 West Short Street.

1932

The heaviest rainfall in the history of the city came on August 2, 1932, when seven and one-half inches fell within seven hours, causing water to stand three feet deep on Main Street. The total property damaged was estimated at more than a million dollars.[1]

Elizabeth M. Simpson's book *Bluegrass Houses and their Traditions* was printed by the Transylvania Press, Lexington. The author's second book, *The Enchanted Bluegrass,* came out in 1938 from the same printer.

The Rev. Alonzo W. Fortune's book, *The Disciples of Kentucky,* was published by the Convention of Christian Churches in Kentucky. Dr. Fortune was pastor of the Central Christian Church.

1933

On March 1, 1933, Governor Ruby Lafoon issued a proclamation declaring a four-day bank holiday for the state of Kentucky, and extended it for six additional days. The failure of banks in Cincinnati and in some northern Kentucky cities was considered the primary cause of the action. The bank holiday spread to all 48 states. The abrupt closing caught many Lexington citizens short of ready cash and created a strained financial situation. Another day was spent in getting permits to open the banks.[2] Finally, on March 14, all Lexington banks opened and business was resumed as usual.

Late in March, Congress legalized the sale of 3.2% beer (classed as non-intoxicating), to become effective at 12:01 A.M., April 7, 1933.[3] Sale of whiskey did not become legal until the 18th Amendment was repealed on December 5, of that year.

The memorial fountain at the north end of Gratz Park was erected with funds left by the noted Kentucky novelist and short-story writer, James Lane Allen, and was dedicated October 15, 1933. The monument was designed by Joseph P. Pollia, New York sculptor, and cost $6,000. The memorial stands on the site of Transylvania's first building.

1934

The end of the interurban traction system began on January 13, 1934, when the motormen went on a strike, and the company not being able to meet its financial obligations was thrown into bankruptcy. Two days later the interurban car system in the Bluegrass came to an end. At the time, the Kentucky Traction & Terminal Company operated both the interurban and the city street cars.

On March 18, 1934, the sale of liquor in Kentucky became legal when Governor Ruby Laffon signed the control act. This ended prohibition through the Volstead Act which had been passed in January, 1919, and had become effective a year later.

On the morning of April 28, 1934, the James E. Pepper Distillery on the Old Frankfort Pike, near the city limits, was destroyed by fire.[4] The gauging room, bottling room, and four warehouses went up in the blaze. Stanley Travis, a night watchman, died in the fire. Loss to the company was $4,500,000 in barreled whiskey, $660,000 in bottled whiskey, and $100,000 in buildings. Financially, this was Lexington's greatest fire loss.

Construction of Midland Avenue, between East Main and East Third streets, was completed by September 9, 1934.

WLAP, the first commercial radio station in Lexington, went on the air in the summer of 1934 with 100 watts of power. The tower consisted of a 100-foot pipe atop the Walton Building at Main Street and the Esplanade. Originally licensed in Louisville in September, 1922 by the Lampton family, the station was acquired by the Virginia Avenue Baptist Church in 1926. Eight years later, Gilmore N. Nunn and his father, J. Lindsay Nunn, purchased the station and moved it to Lexington. Currently, the station operates on a power of 5,000 watts with four 250-foot towers at the southwest corner of the Huffman Mill and Russell Cave pikes, five miles north of Lexington.

On December 1, 1934, the new 12,000-barrel warehouse of the James E. Pepper Distillery at the city limits on the Old Frankfort Pike collapsed, sending 250,000 gallons of whiskey into the streets, gutters and on into Town Branch.

The new post office at the northeast corner of Barr and Limestone streets was officially opened on December 9, 1934. The three-story Bedford limestone building was designed by John T. Gillig and Howard A. Churchill, and erected at a cost of $485,000 by the Penker Construction Company of Cincinnati. The United States District Court and government offices occupy the second and third floors.

1935

Stage-Coach Days in the Bluegrass, by J. Winston Coleman, Jr., was published by the Standard Press, Louisville. A second edition appeared in 1936.

The Kentucky Association Race Track, at Fifth and Race streets, which had been in business since 1826, held its last meeting in the spring of 1933, and the track and grandstand were dismantled in the fall of 1935. Two iron gate posts with "K.A." on them now stand at the entrance to Keeneland Track on the Versailles Pike. A federal housing project (Blue Grass Park) occupies the site of this historic race course.

1937

On January 25 and 26, 1937, more than 1,300 prisoners from the flooded State Penitentiary at Frankfort were brought to Lexington and housed under heavy guard in various buildings. Five hundred prisoners were placed in the old post office, Main and Walnut; 349 at the U. S. Public Service Hospital on the Leestown Pike; 227 in the state highway garage; 225 in the city and county jails; 35 at Kentucky Village, and 36 in the city police station. A barbed-wire barricade was thrown up around the post office, with guards and machine guns placed at strategic points. The prisoners remained here for about two weeks.

The Junior League Horse Show was first held in July, 1937, at the Kentucky Trotting Horse Breeders Association (Fair Grounds), with exhibitors from 20 states. It has grown to be one of the largest outdoor shows in the country, with entries from every state in the Union and Canada. This show features saddle and harness horses and usually runs for a week each July.

Thomas D. Clark's book, *A History of Kentucky,* was published by Prentice-Hall, Inc., in New York. Two later editions have appeared.

1938

Early in January, 1938, motor buses began to replace the electric streetcars. By March 20, 15 new double-door buses were put in the fleet, and by May 6, the number was increased to 22. At that time the company's name was changed from Kentucky Traction & Terminal Company to the Lexington Railway System.

The Carty Building, a four-story, iron-front structure, stood on the

The Carty Building (described above).

southwest corner of Main and Mill streets, on the site of the stockade erected in 1779 by Robert Patterson. A frame building in 1788 replaced the garrison and in 1807, a two-story brick was erected here. This survived until 1871, when the iron-front structure was built; it was razed in May, 1938, and was replaced with a two-story brick structure now on the site.

Dr. John S. Chambers' book, *The Conquest of Cholera,* was published by the MacMillian Company, New York.

Time *magazine called the above building (described at right) "the most orderly of disorderly houses." The house is currently an apartment house.*

The "Red Mile" track at the Fair Grounds is known the country over as the fastest track in the United States. A number of world records have been established on its clay-packed soil. Some of the horses that made history in the days of high-wheeled sulkies were Maude S., Joe Patchen, John R. Gentry, Billy Direct and Robert J — all pacing greats of the 1890s. In October, 1938, Greyhound, a six-year-old trotter, set a world record when he went a mile in 1:55-¼, and in 1966, Bret Hanover, a four-year-old pacer, covered the same distance in 1:55-3/5, a record which still stands. Greyhound's time was not beaten until 1969, when Nevele Pride trotted a mile in 1:54-4/5 at Indianapolis.

1939

Constantine S. Rafinesque, professor of natural sciences and botany at Transylvania University, 1819-1826, died in Philadelphia on September 18, 1840. He was buried in the potters' field where in 1919, Dr. H. C. Mercer placed a stone over his grave. In March, 1924, Rafinesque's remains were removed to Lexington and later "entombed" in a brick burial vault on Derby Day, 1939, in the west crypt of Old Morrison, where he had labored and taught for seven years. The remains of Professor Sauveur F. Bonfils, an early French teacher at Transylvania, were also reinterred there.

Charles R. Staples' book, *The History of Pioneer Lexington* was published by the Transylvania Press, Lexington.

1940

The fine, two-story ante-bellum brick house, The Elms, stood several hundred yards east of the junction of the Harrodsburg Pike and Clay's Mill Road. It was built during the early 1850s for William Leavy, a prominent citizen of Lexington. During its construction, the architect John McMurtry became the owner, and he, in turn, lost the property in 1856. The Elms was constructed of Flemish bond brick, with four tall columns resting on the stone steps running the full length of the porch. In later years this house became an orphanage and then part of the Lafayette High School before it burned in the spring of 1940. Another building has been erected on the site.

White Cottage, a fine brick residence with columns and a recessed portico, stood on the north side of 321 East Short Street a little east of Deweese. It was erected around 1814 on "Out-Lott" No. 43, and Farmer Deweese lived here. General Francis Blair, Jr. of the Union Army was born in the house in 1821. In June, 1889, the Protestant Infirmary (later Good Samaritan Hospital) was established here by the Christ Church Womans' Guild. The author was born here on November 5, 1898. Unoccupied for a number of years, White Cottage fell into decay and was torn down in June, 1940.

Belle Breezing, a well-known Lexington "Madame," conducted a "genteel house" on Megowan Street (now North Eastern Ave.) corner of Wilson. The U. S. Army in 1917 closed down Miss Belle's "resort," and from that time until her death, August 11, 1940,[5] she lived in semi-seclusion amidst the decaying splendor of her once-famous house. *Time* magazine, in its obituary column, described her as "a famous Lexington bawd who ran the most orderly of disorderly houses." She is said to have been the prototype for Belle Watling in *Gone With the Wind.* Belle Breezing is buried in the Calvary Cemetery on West Main Street.

Slavery Times in Kentucky, by J. Winston Coleman, Jr., was published in an edition of 2,000 copies by the University of North Carolina Press, at Chapel Hill. This work was republished in 1970 by the Johnson Reprint Corporation, New York and London, as part of the Basic Afro-American Reprint Library.

The Bluegrass Horse Country, by Joe Jordan, was published by the Transylvania Press, Lexington.

1941

Early Sunday morning, September 28, 1941, Marion Miley, a

During 1940 the old Post Office building at the corner of Walnut and Main streets was razed. The building had earlier been replaced by the Federal Office Building and Post Office on Barr Street.

young golf champion, and her mother, Mrs. Elsa Miley, were attacked by two masked men in their apartment at the Lexington Country Club. Marion was fatally shot in the head and back; her mother was shot three times in the stomach, but lived until October 1. Robbery was the motive for the attack which netted the gunmen less than $150. Robert Anderson, Thomas C. Penney and the groundskeeper Raymond "Skeeter" Baxter were arrested and tried for the crime. All three men died February 23, 1943, in the electric chair at Eddyville Penitentiary.

After the Lexington Opera House on North Broadway was leased to motion-picture interests, Lexington's remaining legitimate attractions moved to the Woodland Park Auditorium and it was there that the last of the road shows played. Among those were Otis Skinner in "Blood and Sand," Richerd Bennett in "The Barker," Earl Carroll's "Vanities," and the musical shows "Student Prince" and "Blossom Time." The last rang down the final curtain at Woodland Auditorium in November, 1941.

1942

Glendower, the low, rambling, one-story brick house, was erected around 1818-25, and three-story square towers on each end were added after the Civil War. Robert Wickliffe, Sr., known as the "Old Duke" and the largest slaveholder in the Bluegrass lived here. Later the property passed to General William Preston who served in the Mexican War, represented Kentucky in Congress, was United States minister to Spain and was a major-general in the Confederate Army. Historic Glendower at the northwest corner of Jefferson and Second streets, was razed in March, 1942. It was replaced by Euphrasia Hall.

On June 4, 1942, exercises were held on the courthouse lawn by the Kentucky Society, Sons of the Revolution, to celebrate the sesqui-centennial of Kentucky's statehood. Lieutenant Governor William Tuck of Virginia delivered the principal address. A bronze marker was unveiled by the society near the Morgan statue to commemorate Kentucky's admission (June 1792) into the federal union as the fifteenth state.

Thomas D. Clark's *The Kentucky* in the Rivers of America series was published by Farrar & Rinehart, New York, 1942. It was republished in 1969 by the Henry Clay Press, Lexington.

1946

On July 22, 1946, parking meters were first used in Lexington. Some motorists reported a number of the meters did not work and other meters were shortchanging parkers by as much as thirty minutes.

Judge Samuel M. Wilson, Kentucky historian, author, and lawyer, died in the Barnes Hospital in St. Louis, Missouri, October 10, 1946, aged 75 years. He was the author (with Temple Bodley) of a four-volume *History of Kentucky* and other works.

Walnut Grove, erected in 1817 by John H. Morton, stood in Maxwelton Court off South Limestone Street and opposite the University of Kentucky's Memorial Hall. Susan Hart Shelby, daughter of Kentucky's first governor, lived here; other occupants have been Dr. James Fishback, Dr. Levi Herr, John A. Prall, and Prof. Arthur M. Miller who deeded the property to the University in 1923. In 1946, the historic house was torn down to make way for the College of the Bible (Lexington Theological Seminary) which moved from the Transylvania campus in 1950 and now occupies the site.

During World War II the Lexington Lions Club sponsored this memorial billboard listing the names of Fayette County casualties of the conflict.

On Nov. 2, 1947, Man o' War died at Faraway Farm. "Big Red" was buried in this giant casket.

1947

On November 4, 1947, Man o' War, often called "Big Red," was laid to rest with appropriate ceremonies at the Faraway Farm on the Huffman Mill Pike. More than 2,000 persons attended the funeral. The horse's colorful groom, Will Harbut, had died a month before. Herbert Heseltine was commissioned to make a life-size statue of the horse, which stands over the grave, surrounded by a moat ten feet wide and four feet deep. Man o' War never raced in Kentucky, and was only defeated once in his career, by Upset.

On November 11, 1948, Norwood Hall at the University of Kentucky burned; the loss was put at $200,000. The building housed the Kentucky Department of Mines and Minerals and other agencies.

1949

A Bibliography of Kentucky History, by J. Winston Coleman, Jr., was published by the University of Kentucky Press, in an edition of 2,500 copies.

The University of Kentucky graduate school was opened to Negro students by a ruling of Federal District Judge H. Church Ford, March 30, 1949.

Dr. Frank L. McVey's book, *The Gates Open Slowly,* was published by the University of Kentucky Press, Lexington.

This year an addition was put on the Phoenix Hotel, originally known as Postlethwait's Tavern, at the southeast corner of Main and Limestone streets.

Gen. Levi Todd built the fine, two-story brick home, Ellerslie, about 1787, on the Richmond Pike opposite No. 1 Reservoir of the city water works. The house was doubled in size, probably in 1792, when 100 acres were added to the Todd estate. Robert S. Todd, father of Mrs. Abraham Lincoln, was born here. When the old residence was razed in December, 1947-January, 1948, it was thought to have been the oldest brick house in Fayette County.

Coach Adolph Rupp of the University of Kentucky and his basketball team of 1947-1948, the Fabulous Five — Ralph Beard, Kenny Rollins, Cliff Barker, Wallace (Wah-Wah) Jones and Alex Groza, won the Southeastern Conference, the NCAA, and the Olympic championship in London, England.

1948

President Harry S. Truman stopped in Lexington on October 1, 1948.[6] He was campaigning for re-election and addressed a group of citizens from the rear of a special C. & O. train on Midland Avenue. He was en route from Louisville to Ashland.

Notes

1. *Lexington Herald,* August 3, 1932.
2. *Lexington Leader,* March 14, 1933.
3. *Lexington Herald,* April 7, 1933.
4. *Ibid.,* April 28, 1934.
5. *Ibid.,* August 13, 1940.
6. *Lexington Herald,* October 1, 1948.

1950-1972

Lexington — Modern City in the Blue Grass

In 1958 the *U. S. News and World Report* included Lexington in its 14 fastest growing cities in America while another national magazine declared Lexington and the Blue Grass to be one of the nation's "most pleasant places to live." Plants built by IBM, Square D, Westinghouse, Dixie Cup, and the many that continue to follow these national corporations which built in Lexington are coupled with other growth like the Spindletop Research Center and the Council of State Governments. National increases in affluence and leisure time make the horse, tobacco, and whiskey industries even more able to maintain their strong positions.

1950

Major General George B. Duncan, a native of Lexington and a graduate of the United States Military Academy, was the first American general officer in World War I to command a sector of the battle front north of Toul, France, January, 1918. He later commanded the 82nd Division from October, 1918 to May, 1919. General Duncan died in Lexington on March 15, 1950.

Memorial Coliseum at the University of Kentucky on Euclid Avenue near Rose Street, was dedicated to the memory of Kentucky's 9,333 dead in World War II on May 30, 1950. The structure cost $4,000,000. Basketball games, as well as commencement exercises, concerts, and other events have been held here, beginning with the 1950-51 season. It replaced the old Alumni Gymnasium still standing near the southeast corner of Limestone Street and Euclid Avenue, which had been dedicated on Thanksgiving Day, 1923, and built at a cost of $100,000.

Epworth Methodist Church started as a mission in 1894 when it erected a small brick meeting house on Rand Avenue near Walnut Street. A larger brick church was built in 1918 at the corner of Walnut and Rand Avenue. The present Epworth building is a more commodious brick church at 1015 North Limestone Street, which was erected at a cost of $310,000 and dedicated October 8, 1950, with the Rev. Warner P. Jones, pastor.

1951

Kentucky upset Oklahoma 13 to 7 in the Sugar Bowl football game on New Year's Day of 1951.

Johnson City School No. 4, at the northwest corner of Limestone and Fourth streets, was erected during the years 1889-1890. It was a large, two-story brick structure with a circular frame tower. School had not been held here for a number of years. During World War II the building was used as a packing plant for electrical and signal corps equipment for overseas shipment from the Lexington Signal Depot at Avon. A fire seriously damaged the building in the fall of 1951, and it was torn down during the ensuing December and January.

Johnson School (described above).

William H. Townsend was the first president of the Kentucky Civil War Round Table and a noted historian.

James F. Hopkins' book, *The University of Kentucky, its Origins and Early Years,* was published by the University of Kentucky Press, Lexington. The author's other book, *A History of the Hemp Industry in Kentucky,* came from the same press this year.

1952

On the morning of February 27, 1952, the R. J. Reynolds Company's storage tobacco warehouse No. 8 was damaged by fire to the extent of $750,000. This building was located off the Versailles Pike near Angliana Avenue. Two nightwatchmen were later convicted of arson.

The Hernando Building, the three-story, stone office building just east of the Phoenix Hotel, was completed about May 2, 1894,[1] and was razed in July, 1952. At one time it housed the city offices, and for many years the Western Union telegraph office occupied the first floor.

In 1952, the Kentucky Wildcats defeated Texas Christian University 20 to 7 in the Cotton Bowl at Dallas, Texas.

1953

At 327 Lafayette Avenue stood the brick burial vault of Gen. George Trotter, Jr., a veteran of the War of 1812, who died in Lexington October 13, 1815. The general, his wife and other relatives were buried in this vault which had been erected on the rear of Trotter's farm, Woodlands, a part of which is now Woodland Park.[2] The last burial here was around 1850. A large quantity of dirt was heaped over the vault, giving it the appearance of an Indian mound. In 1898, a group of boys entered the tomb and carried away the skull and coffin plate of General Trotter, which were later returned. On May 22, 1953, the remains of the family were removed to the Millersburg Cemetery in Bourbon County.

On October 28, 1953, a dozen Central Kentuckians met and organized the Kentucky Civil War Round Table, with William H. Townsend as president. Two weeks later, on November 18, the first dinner meeting was held at the University of Kentucky Student Union with 45 persons present. Dr. Holman Hamilton is the current president; membership is about 535.

1954

President Dwight D. Eisenhower visited Lexington on April 23, 1954. He spoke at the 175th anniversary celebration of Transylvania University and dedicated the new Frances Carrick Thomas Library on the campus.[3]

Central Baptist Hospital at 1740 South Limestone was opened on May 12, 1954. Frankel & Curtis were the architects and Eubank & Steele, general contractors. Phase II of the hospital was added in 1965, and Phase III was completed early in 1972. For the third addition, Watkins-Burrows & Associates were the architects with Foster & Creighton, general contractors. Total cost of the three units amounted to $6,766,568. This made a total of 300 beds, with 31 bassinets.

1955

On March 15, 1955, Lexington's first television station, WLEX-TV, went on the air from 6 P.M. to midnight, with 17 kilowatts power. Currently the station is using a million, four-hundred thousand watts as its power supply. The company's FM radio first went on the air in July, 1969. Principal officers of WLEX are J. Douglas Gay, Jr., Mrs. H. Guthrie Bell, and Harry Barfield.

At the southwest corner of Mill and Second streets stood the John Bradford House, a two-story brick residence thought to have been erected in the mid-1790s. It was the home of Col. Thomas Hart, whose daughter, Lucretia, married Henry Clay here on April 11, 1799. Bradford and his family lived here from 1806 until his death March 21, 1830, and in this house on November 21, 1848, John Hunt Morgan became the husband of Rebecca Gratz Bruce. In later years it was the home of Mrs. Cassius M. Clay and her daughter, Miss Laura Clay. The Bradford house was demolished in March, 1955, to make way for a parking lot.

Still standing at the northwest corner of Mill and Second streets is the Hunt-Morgan House, long known as Hopemont and built in 1814 for John Wesley Hunt, who became the first millionaire in the West. His grandson, General John Hunt Morgan, CSA, spent his early teen-age years here. A two-story, detached building for servants was added behind the service wing, probably in the mid 1840s. Since 1955, the Hunt-Morgan House has been operated as a museum by the Blue Grass Trust for Historic Preservation.

Walter W. Jennings' book, *Transylvania: Pioneer University of the West,* was published by the Pageant Press, New York.

1956

Frazee Hall which housed the history department at the University of Kentucky burned on January 24, 1956. The damage of $202,500 was confined largely to the interior of the building, which was repaired. The building is in use today.

On October 1, 1956, President and Mrs. Dwight D. Eisenhower came to Lexington in the presidential plane "Columbine," which landed at the Blue Grass Airport at 3:05 P.M. The President made a campaign speech at the University of Kentucky at 8:30 P.M. Shortly afterward his party returned to Washington.[4]

A branch plant of the International Business Machines Corporation was started in Lexington and production began on December 26, 1956. Construction continued until 1959 and the plant was dedicated in May of that year. Electric typewriters are the principal product of this large plant at the Newtown Pike and New Circle Road, which covers more than 200 acres and has some 5,800 employees.

1957

Another of Lexington's large industries, the Square D Company, began operations at 1601 Mercer Road in the spring of 1957. The plant, which manufactures electrical distribution equipment, covers 29 acres and has about 1,300 persons employed in the office and factory.

1958

The American Can Company, producers of Dixie Cup and other consumer products, opened for business on Harbison Road in May of 1958. The plant covers fifty acres and employs about 450 persons.

Hopemont, home of John Hunt Morgan (described on next page).

For many years the old Church Street Methodist Church building (erected 1822) on Church Street, between Limestone and Upper, was known as Independence Hall and was the scene of numerous public and civic gatherings. The church building had been used as a Masonic Lodge hall, city hall, Negro church, school and for several business concerns. The venerable edifice was demolished in September, 1958, and a parking lot now occupies the site.

A group of distinguished Kentucky writers and historians gathered at the author's Winburn Farm in 1956. From left: Willard R. Jillson, Holman Hamilton, Hambleton Tapp, Joe Jordan, William H. Townsend, Thomas D. Clark, John Wilson Townsend, and Mr. Coleman.

Built for the Lexington and Ohio Railroad, this station (below) later served the Louisville and Nashville.

1959

Lexington & Ohio Passenger Station, the large, three-story brick station (built in 1835) at the eastern corner of Mill, Water and Vine streets, was demolished in May-June, 1959. This was the second oldest passenger station in the United States; Baltimore & Ohio's Mount Clair station in Baltimore was several years its senior.

Bluegrass Craftsman, by Frances L. S. Dugan and Jacqueline Bull, was published by the University of Kentucky Press.

The cornerstone of the new St. Joseph Hospital at Waller Avenue and Harrodsburg Pike was laid May 11, 1958, and the $5,600,000 building was completed and occupied on June 21, 1959. George Roth, Cincinnati, was the architect; the contractor was Foster & Creighton. A new wing completed in 1971, brings the bed complement to 440. Fourteen acres are involved in the hospital proper. The old High Oaks Sanitarium building, formerly a privately owned institution, was razed to make way for the new wing.

1960

Lafayette Chapter, Sons of the American Revolution, was organized here on March 25, 1960, with James F. Miller, first president. The present membership is between 50 and 60. The women's organization of the SAR, the DAR, has five chapters in Lexington: Captain John McKinley, Lexington, Transylvania, Captain John Waller, and Bryan Station.

The Meadows, a commodious, two-story brick house, stood about 600-700 feet north of East Loudoun Avenue, opposite Magoffin Street. Dr. Elisha Warfield built the house in the early 1830s. Here, in February, 1833, his daughter, Mary Jane Warfield, was married to Cassius M. Clay, noted anti-slavery worker and later ambassador to Russia. The famous racehorse Lexington was born in Dr. Warfield's stable here in 1850. One hundred years later, a subdivision grew up on each side of the driveway leading to the Warfield house, and in September, 1960, the building was razed.

Ground-breaking ceremonies for the Albert B. Chandler Medical Center on Rose Street were held in December, 1957, and the building was dedicated in September, 1960. The University of Kentucky Hospital, the College of Medicine, and the College of Dentistry opened two years later, in September, 1962. Total cost of the buildings was $27.8 million, of which state funds provided $17 million and about $10 million came from federal appropriations.

1961

The Shriners' Mosque at 326 Southland Drive was dedicated on August 5, 1961, with Imperial Potentate Leon M. Porter, the principal speaker. John F. Wilson was the architect; Robert D. Short the contractor. About four acres of ground were purchased; the building cost around $123,000.

The Fayette County Court House, recently remodeled at a cost of $740,000, was opened with ceremony on October 20, 1961.

Union Station was razed in 1960 and it was replaced by a parking garage and office space for securities dealers and state offices.

Betty Gail Brown, of Lexington, a 19-year-old student at Transylvania University, was killed around midnight on October 26, 1961, in her car on the circular drive in front of Old Morrison. Several suspects were arrested and one tried, but no verdict was reached. This remains one of Lexington's unsolved murder cases.

Neville Hall, built in 1891 on the University of Kentucky campus, burned and was a total loss. The building was named for Professor "Jack" Neville, a long-time professor of Latin and Greek at the school.

Ante Bellum Houses of the Bluegrass, by Clay Lancaster, was published by the University of Kentucky Press, Lexington.

1962

On January 1, 1960, a group from Immanuel Baptist Church at High and Woodland Avenue, purchased 22 acres of ground and erected a large building at a cost of $756,700, which was dedicated on July 1, 1962. The church stands at 3100 Tates Creek Pike, several hundred yards south of Mt. Tabor Road. The remaining group from Immanuel Baptist built the Central Baptist Church at 1644 Nicholasville Road. The original Immanuel Church then became the Woodland Avenue Baptist Church, its present designation.

On July 22, 1962, the Calvary Baptist Church congregation moved into a new brick building at the southeast corner of Rodes Avenue and High Street, erected at a cost of $910,000. The new church, which required two years to build, was designed by Lexington architects Clay Brock and Ernst Johnson. It is of Georgian Colonial architecture, with a seating capacity of around 1,800 persons. The sanctuary is 94 feet long and 68 feet wide, and the cross on the tower is 170 feet above the sidewalk. The Rev. Franklin D. Owen has been the minister since August, 1954.

John J. Crittenden, by Albert D. Kirwan, was published by the University of Kentucky Press, Lexington.

1963

One of Lexington's most tragic fires occurred on January 21, 1963, when the Kentucky Food Stores warehouse on Delaware Avenue was destroyed by fire. Four of the firm's executives, W. L. Murray, Herbert McGuire, Carl H. Morgan and Conn Trimble, lost their lives in the blaze which caused nearly a million dollars damage.[5]

The Drake Hotel, which had also been known as the Ashland House and the Reed Hotel, was razed in May 1962. The building was located at 315-17 West Short Street.

Thorn Hill, a 12-room Gothic Revival house, stood at the southeast corner of Limestone and Fifth streets. The quaint two-story structure was owned by John W. Hunt, who sold the property to Joseph C. Breckinridge in 1815, recording in the deed that it "was erected on the first day of April, 1812." Gen. John C. Breckinridge, CSA, was born here January 21, 1821, and spent his teenage years in the house. Charlton Hunt, Lexington's first mayor was also born here. During the 1850s, Thorn Hill was remodeled and enlarged and the two-story front section was added. The historic old house was demolished in April, 1963, and an apartment building now occupies the site.

The Trane Company, manufacturer of air-conditioning, heating and air-handling equipment, went into production on Mercer Road in 1963. At the present time there are approximately 750 employees and the plant, near the New Circle Road, covers 62.8 acres of ground.

1964

In 1860, William R. Fleming purchased an 11-acre tract to the west of Rose Street, between High and Maxwell, and engaged local architect John McMurtry to design his house. McMurtry produced an imposing, three-story brick building with a tower. Fleming was unable to complete the villa and the place was sold in 1867 for $35,000 to Robert R. Stone who named it Lyndhurst after his Canadian home. In recent years the lawn of the house was taken up by a subdivision and the old house itself was razed in April, 1964, and replaced with an apartment building.

Ingelside, a two-story Gothic Revival house with four towers, stood near the city limits on the west side of the Harrodsburg Pike, at 600 Gibson Park. The 15-room mansion was designed and erected by John McMurtry for Henry Boone Ingels, at a cost of $25,000. The date of construction, 1852, was cut on a stone and set high up on the principal tower of this Bluegrass "castle." Ingelside was demolished in June, 1964, to make way for a trailer park.

A record low temperature of 22 degrees below zero was observed in Lexington on Thursday, January 24, 1963. This shattered the earlier record of -20 on February 13, 1889. Driving was hazardous in both city and county. A total of 27 accidents, with no serious injuries, was reported.[6]

On June 24, 1964, the Felix Memorial Baptist Church at 239-41 East Fifth Street became the Parkway Baptist Church and the same year the congregation erected a new church at 1915 North Broadway, on the west side of the Paris Pike. The church prop-

Thorn Hill (described above left) was twice owned by John W. Hunt and the second time his son Charlton was born here.

Ingelside (described at left).

erty on East Fifth Street was sold to the Shiloh Baptist Church, a Negro congregation, which continues to occupy the building as a place of worship.

Hundred Proof, "a collection of Salt River Sketches and Memoirs of the Bluegrass," by William H. Townsend, was published by the University of Kentucky Press. Bill Townsend, a Civil War historian, attorney, Lincoln authority and raconteur, is probably best remembered for his memorable address on Cassius M. Clay before the Chicago Civil War Round Table on October 17, 1952. The speech was recorded and has been sought all over the United States. Townsend died in Lexington on July 25, 1964, and is buried in the Lexington Cemetery.

Mechanical Hall at the University of Kentucky, later known as Anderson Hall, was razed during August-September, 1964. Erected in 1891, Mechanical Hall, with several buildings erected later, housed all the engineering shops, class rooms, and offices of the College of Engineering. This was replaced with a seven-story building connected with the Engineering Quadrangle so as to form a central complex.

The Robert M. Sirkle Lodge No. 954, F. & A. M., was chartered October 21, 1964, with Dr. Robert M. Sirkle, first master. This is the third Masonic lodge currently operating in Lexington.

1965

Sudduth Goff, portrait painter, was born August 6, 1887, at Eminence, Kentucky, son of Thomas and Mary Sudduth Goff. He studied at Transylvania University, the Cincinnati Art Academy, and the Museum of Fine Arts at Boston. Goff died February 7, 1965 in Lexington and was buried in the Winchester Cemetery.

On February 22, 1965, the University of Kentucky celebrated its centennial with appropriate exercises in Memorial Coliseum. Distinguished alumni awards were given to 81 living alumni and 24 were presented to families of the deceased. Dr. John W. Oswald, the school's president, conferred the honorary degree of Doctor of Laws on President Lyndon B. Johnson, who delivered the principal address. The day's activities were concluded with a nine-course dinner in the evening at Spindletop Hall on the Iron Works Pike.

Hawthorn, the two-story, red brick ante-bellum home of Orlando F. Payne, former mayor of Lexington and representative to the Confederate Constitutional Convention at Russellville in 1861, stood on the northwest corner of Limestone and Seventh streets. It was demolished in April, 1965. A junk yard occupies the site.

Police reported the death of Mary Marrs Cawein, wife of Dr. Madison Cawein III, at their home at 306 Chinoe Road on July 5, 1965. This still remains an unsolved case.

The Kentuckian Hotel, at the northwest corner of East High Street and Harrison Avenue Viaduct, was razed during the summer of 1965, along with three buildings on the west side. They were torn down to make way for a proposed 14-story Sheraton-Kentuckian Motor Inn, which did not materialize.

On November 15, 1953, 42 persons from Immanuel Baptist Church met to organize Central Baptist Church and Dr. Clyde Chapman was called as the first pastor. The new congregation acquired five acres at 1644 South Limestone and met there during the years 1954 to 1965 in a temporary sanctuary. The Rev. Homer D. Carter became the second pastor in October, 1957. The cornerstone of a new brick church with six columns was laid February 28, 1965, and the building was dedicated September 26, 1965. The structure, with a seating capacity of 800, was erected at a cost of $725,000. William A. Bryant was the architect, and the general contractor was the A. & P. Construction Company of Lexington.

Charles G. Talbert's book, *The University of Kentucky, The Maturing Years,* was published by the University of Kentucky Press, Lexington.

1966

Another Lexington bank, the Bank of Lexington, was opened for business on June 1, 1966, at 311 East Main Street. Forrest E. Hansen was first president and former Governor Bert T. Combs was chairman of the board. Capital stock was set at one million dollars.

The large, four-story St. Joseph Hospital building on the south side of West Second Street between Jefferson and Georgetown, which had been abandoned in June, 1959, was razed in May-July, 1966.

The Kirwan-Blanding Housing Complex at the University of Kentucky was opened for occupancy in September, 1966. The twin towers (23 floors) were named for Dr. Albert D. Kirwan and Miss Sarah G. Blanding, and have a housing capacity for nearly 2,700 students. Edward Durrell Stone & Associates of New York, were the architects; Foster & Creighton, Nashville, were the general contractors. The total cost of the complex, including site development, landscaping, and related work, came to $22 million.

On the west side of the Nicholasville Pike, several hundred yards south of Southland Drive stood Alleghan Hall, a fine example of Greek Revival architecture. This large, two-story brick building with massive columns, was erected in 1857 by William B. Pettit; later, in 1887 the property passed to Professor A. N. Gordon who conducted a noted boys school here until 1900. In 1909, the house was owned by Mrs. C. W. Burt. On December 6, 1966, the historic house was demolished and business places now occupy the site.

1967

On Tuesday afternoon at 4:30 P.M., April 3, 1967, nine men lost their lives in an airplane accident near Blue Grass Airport, six miles west on Lexington on the Versailles Pike. Those who died in the crash were: Dr. Silvio O. Navarro, Dr. Richard Schweet, Dr. Rinaldo C. Simonini, and Dr. Jerome C. Cohn, University of Kentucky professors; G. Reynolds Watkins, a local consulting engineer, and the pilot, Robert Yonk, all of Lexington; Max Horn, St. Louis, Robert Salop, Austin, Texas, and Richard H. Southwood, Buffalo Grove, Illinois. Overloading of the two-engine chartered plane was said to have been the cause of the crash.

Blue Grass Lodge No. 956, F. & A. M., was chartered October 18, 1967, with Thomas W. Horine, first master. Currently this is the fourth Masonic lodge operating in the city.

Historic Kentucky, by J. Winston Coleman, Jr., was published by Henry Clay Press, Lexington. The second edition followed in 1968, and the third in 1969.

The large and handsome Christ the King Catholic Church on Providence and Colony Road in Chevy Chase was built during the years 1966-67, at a cost of $1,200,000. Edward Schulte was the architect; the Lexington Lumber & Supply Company were the general contractors. The windows are of sculptured glass made in Chartres, France. The church property, including the parochial school and the playground includes a total of ten acres. Seating capacity of this Bedford stone building is estimated at 1,200 persons. The Rev. Garland O'Neill was the pastor at the time the church was constructed.

1968

On June 2, 1968, Lexington's newest television station, WBLG, went on the air as an affiliate of the ABC network. This station is said to have the highest television tower in Kentucky.

On March 1, 1961, the First National Bank & Trust Company and the Security Trust Company merged. Several suits were filed opposing the consolidation. After numerous hearings in the district courts and four in the U. S. Supreme Court, the two banks were declared officially merged on October 18, 1968, under the name First Security National Bank and Trust Company, making it the largest bank in Central Kentucky.

The New Circle Road around the city, which had been built in sections beginning in the early 1950s, was finished and officially dedicated on December 17, 1968, at the Richmond Pike intersection. Mayor Charles Wylie cut the ribbon, and other officials participated in the ceremonies. The road around the city is nineteen and three-quarter miles long.

After the Union Station on East Main Street was razed in 1960, the C. & O. Railroad used its old freight depot at Rose and Water streets for a passenger station. When the city prepared to remove the downtown tracks in 1968, the C. & O. erected a small passenger station at 1008 Delaware Avenue. The last train ran from the depot on Rose Street to the new Delaware station on December 17, 1968.

William B. Floyd's book, *Jouett-Bush-Frazer: Early Kentucky Artists,* was privately published by the author; printed by the Transylvania Printing Company, Lexington.

Old Morrison, Transylvania's historic administration building, was severely gutted by fire in January, 1969.

1969

The Connie R. Griffith Manor, a ten-story federal housing project for senior citizens, was erected at a cost of $2 million on the site of the old St. Joseph Hospital, during the years 1967-1969. The Manor opened for business on June 5, 1969, and is located on the south side of West Second Street, between Jefferson and Georgetown streets.

The Patterson Office Tower and White Hall Classroom Building at the University of Kentucky, were opened for occupancy on September 1, 1969. This construction necessitated razing President Patterson's house and White Hall both built in 1882, and the small Carnegie library erected in 1907. Ernst Johnson and Byron F. Romanowitz were the architects for the 19-story tower and the classroom building, which were constructed by Foster & Creighton. The cost of the project was $12 million, including site development.

Famous Kentucky Duels, by J. Winston Coleman, Jr., was republished in an expanded edition by the Henry Clay Press, Lexington. The book was orginally printed in 1953 by the Roberts Printing Company, Frankfort, in an edition of 400 copies.

The Great Elm Tree, by Frances K. Swinford and Rebecca S. Lee, was published by the Faith House Press, Lexington.

1970

On May 6, 1970, students on the University of Kentucky campus rioted and burned the ROTC building on Euclid Avenue. Governor Louie B. Nunn sent in National Guard troops and state police to preserve order and protect students and buildings.

The new Henry Clay High School, at the corner of Lakeshore Drive and Fontaine Road, was opened for students in September, 1970. Ground was broken on a 55-acre campus for the school on October 1, 1968. Lexington architects Ernst Johnson and Byron Romanowitz designed the structure. The building cost $5 million, and the grounds, athletic fields, lighting and parking, another $6 million, making a total outlay of $11 million. This school replaced the old two-story red brick Henry Clay High at the northeast corner of East Main and Walton Avenue, erected in 1927, which is still standing.

Originally known as Cane Run, the Italianate villa Glengarry, stood three miles north of Lexington on the Newtown Pike. It was designed by Major Thomas Lewinski and erected in 1854 for Alexander Brand, a wealthy hemp manufacturer. The house, a two-story brick, with three-story tower, passed to the Joseph C. Anderson family in the mid-1880s and the name was changed to Glengarry. This fine ante-bellum residence was destroyed by fire on the evening of February 16, 1970.

During the summer and fall of 1970, Henry Clay's law office, immediately north of the First Presbyterian Church on Mill Street, was restored. The church sold the ground to the Commonwealth of Kentucky for the sum of $24,500, and a public-spirited citizen gave $40,000 to restore the quaint little brick office which Clay used about 1803 to 1807, and where he most likely interviewed Aaron Burr before taking his case for treason which was tried in Frankfort. This is the only remaining one of several offices Mr. Clay had in Lexington.

1971

J. D. Purcell Company, a long-time department store at 320 West Main Street, on the site of the first capital of Kentucky, went out of business January 1, 1971. The company owned and occupied a five-story brick building on the south side of Main, between Mill and Broadway.

On January 19, 1971, Lexington Consistory of the Ancient and Accepted Scottish Rite of Freemasonry was established "under dispensation" in Lexington. On Saturday, May 15, Scottish Rite degrees were conferred on the first class of 408 candidates at the Leestown Junior High School, a mile and a half west of Lexington on the Leestown Pike.

Old Morrison at Transylvania University, which was severly damaged by fire on the evening of January 29, 1969, with a loss estimated at a half million dollars, was rededicated with appropriate ceremonies on the afternoon of May 9, 1971. Dr. Raymond F. McLain, former president of the University, delivered the principal address. During the afternoon a highway marker was unveiled on the campus giving the history of Old Morrison. The historic building, erected in 1833-34, was completely restored after the fire. It has been designated a Registered National Historic Landmark.

On Wednesday, March 17, 1971, President Richard M. Nixon came to Lexington to deliver the eulogy at graveside services for Whitney M. Young, Jr., director of the National Urban League. Young, who was born in Kentucky, died March 11 in Lagos, Nigeria, and was buried in the local Greenwood Cemetery. Several weeks later his body was removed to a cemetery in New Rochelle, New York. Nixon was the tenth president to have visited the Bluegrass Capital while in office.

The Rev. Billy Grahm, famed evangelist, began a four-day crusade in Lexington on Sunday afternoon, April 25, 1971. Meetings were held in the University of Kentucky Memorial Coliseum and the football stadium across the street. During the meeting 77,500 persons attended the services. Several movie and television stars and a 1,500-voice choir appeared on the program.

Lexington's last two passenger trains, the east and west George Washington of the Chesapeake & Ohio Railroad, were discontinued May 1, 1971. The eastbound George Washington left Lexington at 5:30 P.M., April 30, for Washington, D. C., and the last westbound train for Frankfort and Louisville at 8:05 A.M., May 1. With the exception of periods of nationwide rail strikes, this was the first time in 139 years Lexington had been without a passenger train.

On June 14, 1969, Trinity Baptist Church burned at 1675 Strader Drive with a loss of $500,000. The cause of the fire was not determined. A new concrete slab structure was erected on the site at a cost of $700,000 and opened for worship on Sunday, October 3, 1971, with Rev. Robert Brown, pastor.

A new one-way traffic plan in downtown Lexington went into effect on Thursday, June 24, with the opening of the new Vine Street through the Urban Renewal area. Main Street from Midland to Spring was declared one-way west and Vine Street was officially opened as a one-way street east from Spring to Midland.

On June 28, the 187-year-old Adam Rankin house of logs covered with clapboard, was moved intact in one day from its original location, 215 West High Street, to 317 South Mill Street. It is said to be the oldest house standing in Lexington. The house was restored and sold with use restrictions by the Blue Grass Trust for Historic Preservation.

In the first week of August, workmen began the erection of the new Citizens-Union National Bank & Trust Company building in the block bounded by High, Upper, Vine and Mill streets. The new building is an eight-story structure of steel and concrete and is scheduled for occupancy early in 1973. Part of the building occupies the original site of the Adam Rankin house at 215 West High Street.

Located three miles south of Lexington on the west side of the Tates Creek Pike, Kirklevington, a two-story brick mansion, was built in 1853 by Hamilton A. Headley on his 415-acre farm. The house had much in common with Waveland and had a fine doorway, complete with transom and side lights. In 1878, Joseph Clark became owner of the property and four years later it passed to Archival L. Hamilton who named it Kirklevington after a breed of sheep. Unoccupied for several years and greatly damaged by vandals, the fine Greek Revival house was demolished during the summer of 1971.

During August and September, three of Lexington's older elementary schools were torn down to make way for new buildings on the same site. These were Maxwell School, at the southwest corner of Maxwell Street and Woodland Avenue; Ashland School on the southwest corner of Ashland and Cramer, and Harrison School on the west side of Bruce Street, near Second Street. All three buildings were two-story brick structures.

On October 28, *Kentucky: A Pictorial History,* was published by the University Press of Kentucky, with J. Winston Coleman, Jr.,

Kirklevington (described below left).

editor. The first edition of 20,000 copies sold out two weeks after publication; the second edition of 40,000 copies appeared in March, 1972.

1972

On April 12, ground was broken for the new home of the First Security National Bank & Trust Company at Main and Walnut streets. The 15-story, 230-foot-high bank and office building will occupy approximately the western half of the block bounded by Main, Walnut, Short and the Esplanade. It is scheduled to be ready for occupancy within two years. The general contractor is the Pankow Construction Company, of Los Angeles and San Francisco, and the architectural firm for the project is Welton Becket & Associates, of New York and Houston.

Lexington's newest and seventh bank, the Bank of the Blue Grass, was organized in mid-April, 1972, at 101 East High Street, with Charles H. Jett, Jr., president and C. H. Jett, III, vice-president and cashier. This banking institution was formed when the corporate charter of the Preferred Thrift and Loan Plan, Inc., was amended and a state bank charter was obtained.

Transylvania Printing Company, a century-old business in Lexington began operations early in 1872, at 49-51 East Main Street, corner of Wrenn Court. The firm moved in 1888 to No. 10 East Main (now 258 West Main), opposite Cheapside, where it remained until 1926 when it was relocated at 106-08 North Upper Street. It moved to its present location at 139 West Short Street in 1951.

Plans are being made to construct a large concrete stadium on the Experiment Station grounds, south of Cooper Drive and east of South Limestone. It will have 50,000 sideline seats and 8,000 end zone seats. The cost of the new stadium is put at 11 million dollars, and is expected to be completed by the fall of 1973. Approximately 85 acres will be covered by the stadium, access roads and parking facilities. This structure will replace the old football stadium on Euclid Avenue near Rose, which was built in 1924. The firm of Finch-Heery, Atlanta, with Lexington architects Johnson and Romanowitz, will design the new stadium.

Lexington's second oldest business firm, the W. R. Milward Mortuary, was established in 1825 by Joseph Milward, who opened a cabinet shop. He became one of Kentucky's finest craftsmen and because of his trade soon became active in funeral service. Today, the 147-year-old firm, with locations at 159 North Broadway and 391 Southland Drive, is owned and operated by members of the fourth and fifth generation, W. Emmet Milward and his son, Robert E. Milward.

Late in June workmen began razing the three-story brick building, first known as the Pilgrim Baptist Church and later as the Upper Street Baptist Church, at the southwest corner of Market and Church streets. This large structure had been remodeled after 1905; a new front was added and for a number of years it housed the offices and plant of the Fayette Home Telephone Company. In recent years the building was converted into business offices and known as the Exchange Building. A parking lot occupies the site.

Notes

1. *Lexington Morning Transcript,* May 6, 1894.
2. *Lexington Herald,* May 23, 1953.
3. *The Courier-Journal,* April 21, 1954.
4. *Lexington Leader,* September 28, 1956.
5. *Ibid.,* January 22, 1963.
6. *Lexington Herald,* January 24, 1963.

POSTSCRIPT —

On November 7, 1972, as the first edition of *The Squire's SKETCHES OF LEXINGTON* was being printed, the citizens of Lexington and Fayette County voted by a 2-1 margin to approve a merged form of city-county urban government. The first such governmental reorganization in the Commonwealth, the change was prompted since Lexington was nearing the population that would require that it become a first class city and thereby fall under laws written for the city of Louisville. At the time of the merger Lexington's mayor was H. Foster Pettit and the city commissioners were Dr. J. Farra Van Meter, Scott Yellman, William Hoskins, and Richard Vimont. The Fayette County judge was Robert Stephens and the county commissioners were J. D. Marshall, J. W. Lynch, and Doc Ferrell.

Lexington's future seems even brighter since the merger was designed to ease the growing burden on taxpayers, relate taxes to services received, and provide a highly visible, accessible and representative system of local government.

The Editors

Bibliography

Beers, D. G. and J. Lanagan, *Atlas of Bourbon, Clark, Fayette, Jessamine and Woodford Counties, Ky.* Philadelphia, D. G. Beers & Co., 1877.

Brown, Samuel R., *The Western Gazetteer; or Emigrants Directory.* Auburn, N.Y., H. C. Southwick, 1817.

Clark, Thomas D., *A History of Kentucky.* New York, Prentice-Hall, 1937.

__________ *The Kentucky.* Lexington, Henry Clay Press, 1969.

Clay, Cassius M., *The Life of Cassius Marcellus Clay.* Cincinnati, J. Fletcher Brennan, 1886.

Coleman, J. Winston, Jr., *Famous Kentucky Duels,* Lexington, Henry Clay Press, 1969.

__________ *Historic Kentucky.* Lexington, Henry Clay Press, 1967.

__________ *Lexington During the Civil War.* Lexington, Henry Clay Press, 1868.

__________ *Kentucky: A Pictorial History.* Lexington, University Press of Kentucky, 1971.

__________ *Masonry in the Bluegrass.* Lexington, Transylvania Press, 1933.

__________ *Slavery Times in Kentucky.* Chapel Hill, University of North Carolina Press, 1940.

__________ *Stage-Coach Days in the Bluegrass.* Louisville, Standard Press, 1935.

__________ *The Court Houses of Lexington.* Lexington, Privately printed, 1937.

Collins, Richard H., *History of Kentucky.* Covington, Collins & Co., 1874.

Conkwright, Bessie T., *Little Tours among History Shrines in and about Lexington.* Lexington, Lexington Public Library, 1925. (Pamphlet).

Crum, Mabel Tyree, *History of Lexington Theaters from the Beginning to 1860.* 2 vols. Ph.D. thesis, University of Kentucky Library, 1956.

Dupre, Huntley, *Rafinesque in Lexington, 1819-1826.* Lexington, Bur Press, 1945.

Fayette County Court — Order books, wills and deeds.

Floyd, William B., *Jouett-Bush-Frazer: Early Kentucky Artists.* Lexington, Privately published by the author, 1968.

Fortune, Alonzo W., *The Disciples in Kentucky.* St. Louis, The Bethany Press, 1932.

Hall, Charles G., *The Cincinnati Southern Railway.* Cincinnati, The McDonald Press, 1902.

Hening, William W., *The Statutes at Large; Being a Collection of All the Laws of Virginia, 1619-1792.* 13 vols. Richmond, Va., R. & W. Bartow, 1819.

Harrison, Ida W., *Memoirs of William Temple Withers.* Boston, The Christian Publishing Co., 1924.

Herr, Kincaid, *The Louisville & Nashville Railroad.* Louisville, L. & N. Magazine, 1943.

Hill, West T., Jr., *The Theater in Early Kentucky.* Lexington, The University Press of Kentucky, 1971.

Hopkins, James F., *The University of Kentucky: Origin and Early Years.* Lexington, The University of Kentucky Press, 1951.

Jennings, Walter W., *Transylvania: Pioneer University of the West.* New York, Pageant Press, 1955.

Jillson, Willard R., *An Historical Bibliography of Lexington, Kentucky.* Frankfort, The Perry Publishing Co., 1947.

———, "The Founding of Lexington, Kentucky." *The Filson Club History Quarterly,* October, 1929.

Kentucky General Assembly — *Acts.*

Knight, Thomas A., and Nancy L. Greene, *Country Estates of the Blue Grass.* Cleveland, The Burton Printing Co. 1904.

Lancaster, Clay, *Ante Bellum Houses of the Bluegrass.* Lexington, University of Kentucky Press, 1961.

——— *Back Streets and Pine Trees.* Lexington, Bur Press, 1956.

Leavy, William A., "A Memoir of Lexington and Its Vicinity." Manuscript in the Transylvania University Library.

Lexington Leader, Fiftieth Anniversary Edition, June 30, 1938.

Littell, William, *The Statute Law of Kentucky.* 5 vols. Frankfort, Printed by William Hunter, 1809-1819.

Phoenix Hotel, circa 1890.

McCullough, Samuel D., *Reminiscences of Lexington.* Manuscript, Lexington Public Library.

Milward, Burton, *The First One Hundred Years of the Transylvania Printing Company.* Lexington, Transylvania Printing Company, 1972.

Newcomb, Rexford, *Architecture in Old Kentucky.* Urbana, University of Illinois Press, 1953.

Parrish, Gladys V., *The History of Female Education in Lexington and Fayette County.* M.A. thesis, University of Kentucky Library, 1932.

Perrin, William H., *History of Fayette County, Kentucky.* Chicago, O. L. Baskin & Company, 1882.

Peter, Robert, *A Brief History of Lexington and Transylvania University.* Lexington, 1854. (Pamphlet).

Peter, Robert and Johanna Peter, *Transylvania University; its Origin, Rise, Decline and Fall.* Louisville, John P. Morton and Company, 1896.

Ranck, George W., *A Review of Lexington, Kentucky, as She Is.* New York, John Lethem, 1887.

——— *Guide to Lexington, Kentucky.* Lexington, Transylvania Printing Company, 1883.

——— *History of Lexington, Kentucky.* Cincinnati, Robert Clarke & Company, 1872.

Sanders, Robert S., *Annals of the First Presbyterian Church, Lexington, Kentucky.* Louisville, The Dunn Press, 1959.

——— *History of the Second Presbyterian Church, Lexington, Kentucky.* Lexington, Second Presbyterian Church, 1965.

Simpson, Elizabeth M., *Bluegrass Houses and Their Traditions.* Lexington, Transylvania Press, 1932.

———— *The Enchanted Bluegrass.* Lexington, Transylvania Press, 1938.

Smith, Elizabeth K., and Mary L. Didlake, *Historical Sketch of Christ Church Cathedral, Lexington, Ky.* Lexington, Transylvania Printing Co., 1898. Republished as *Christ Church, 1796-1946,* Lexington, 1946.

Smith, J. Soule, *Art Work of the Blue Grass Region of Kentucky.* Oshkosh, Wis., Art Photogravure Company, 1898.

Staples, Charles R., "The Amusements and Diversions of Early Lexington." 36 pages. Transcript copy in University of Kentucky Library.

———— *The History of Pioneer Lexington.* Lexington, Transylvania Press, 1939.

Stevenson, Dwight E., *Lexington Theological Seminary.* St. Louis, The Bethany Press, 1964.

Swinford, Frances E., and Rebecca S. Lee, *The Great Elm Tree.* Lexington, Faith House Press, Lexington, 1969.

Talbert, Charles G., *The University of Kentucky: The Maturing Years.* Lexington, University of Kentucky Press, 1965.

The Church Record. New York, The Church Record Publishing Co. 1897.

The Morning Herald. "Easter Review of Lexington Churches." Easter, 1901.

Townsend, William H., *Lincoln and His Wife's Home Town.* Indianapolis, Bobbs-Merrill Company, 1929.

Van Deusen, Glyndon G., *The Life of Henry Clay.* Boston, Little Brown & Company, 1937.

Walker, Tom L., *History of the Lexington Post Office, from 1794 to 1901.* Lexington, E. D. Veach, 1901.

Wilson, Samuel M., and others, *Kentucky in Retrospect.* Frankfort, Kentucky Historical Society, 1942, 1967.

W.P.A. Writers, *Kentucky: A Guide to the Bluegrass State.* New York, Harcourt, Brace and Company, 1939.

———— *Lexington and the Bluegrass Country.* Lexington, The Commercial Printing Company, 1938.

Index

F

G

H

I

K

L

M

N

O

P

R

S

T

U

Y

W